FROM SORE SOLES
to a
SOARING SOUL

....

*Changing My Life One Step at a Time
on the Camino De Santiago*

BLAINE A. RADA

Print ISBN 978-1-54397-508-6 | ebook ISBN 978-1-54397-509-3

Dedication

Dedicated to those who seek to transform their lives.
I honor your journey.

CONTENTS

PREFACE

I never intended to write this book, but life had other plans.

As I walked the Camino de Santiago, I made notes of my insights and observations, planning to write a more complete summary so I'd have a written record, knowing my memory of the events would fade over time. I also thought my family and a few friends and colleagues would be interested in reading about my journey.

Several months passed after returning home before I reviewed my notes and began writing. In the meantime, I'd shared stories from my adventure with dozens of people, and many of them wanted to know more, and specifically were interested in reading whatever I ended up writing.

As a professional speaker and trainer, I started sharing bits of my Camino experience in my presentations, and again found that people were curious and wanted to hear more. Unlike most of the subjects I speak about, this one connected with people on a very personal level. This motivated me to get busy with the writing, still thinking this would just end up being a document I'd email to friends and family.

As I got into the writing process, I realized it was the largest writing project I'd ever attempted, and that I had a short book in the making. The thought of it now as a book pressured me to create something "significant." I felt perhaps this effort needed to be bigger than just my walk across Spain.

But how? Should I infuse my story with lessons about business, something that would appeal to a broader audience? As I tried to do this, it became clear that was not my purpose. I simply needed to write a daily account of my trek, one step at a time, just as the Camino had been for me.

The Camino de Santiago is a profoundly personal experience for each pilgrim on the path. In these pages, I have shared mine with you, in the hope that you will have your own personal experience in reading it.

ACKNOWLEDGEMENTS

I don't believe we accomplish anything of significance by ourselves. I'd like to thank a few people who've had a considerable influence on me, especially related to my walk across Spain.

For as long as I can remember, my mother has showered me with love and believed in me. We had many adventures together as I was growing up, and I owe some of my adventurous spirit to her. Thanks for the many memories, Mom. I love you.

My father, father-in-law, mother-in-law, and stepmom have shown me how to live life with intention, discipline, and kindness.

My children, Thaddeus and Sequoia, have given me the greatest privilege, responsibility, and joy of my life, being a parent. They've taken the strengths and weaknesses I've shared by my example and made their lives their own. I hope you know how proud I am to be your father.

There are of course, many other friends, family, and colleagues who have influenced me in ways they'll never know. I admire and appreciate all of you. A special thank you to those who read earlier versions of this manuscript and made it better with their suggestions.

To my editor and writing coach, Kelly Joy Simmons, thank you for believing I had something of value to share with a larger audience than I imagined, and for helping me get to the finish line.

Finally, there's one person who I credit with transforming my life in every way possible. Jacki, you're my soulmate and best friend, and you inspire me to keep becoming a better version of myself. I especially appreciate that you love me even when I fall short of who I'm capable of being. I love you more!

PAY ATTENTION
TO INTENTION

"Do you like going for long walks?"

Being asked this question by a fellow pilgrim, or *peregrino*, a few days into my month-long journey walking 500 miles across northern Spain seems ridiculous. And then I realize it's a brilliant question. It seeks to answer why someone would embark on such a challenge.

The *Camino de Santiago* is a 500-mile pilgrimage from Saint-Jean-Pied-de-Port in France to the cathedral in Santiago de Compostela in Galicia, Spain. The Camino became more popular with Americans in 2010 with the release of the movie *The Way*, but it's been walked by millions of people for over 1,200 years. There are as many ways to walk the Camino as there are people who do it. What's consistent is that ordinary people are doing something extraordinary.

Honestly, I don't like walking.

Walks with my wife are pleasurable because it gives us quality time together, but the walking itself isn't that enjoyable for me. I've been a runner for over thirty-five years and I'd much rather run than walk. The first time I did a ten-mile walk to prepare for the Camino, I hated it.

Why would I walk across Spain if I don't like walking? When I first learned about the Camino from the movie *The Way*, I simply knew it was something I would eventually do.

Several years later I decided it was time, and I booked my flights a year before I would take the trip. Over the course of that year I didn't think much about why I was doing it, but when I started to prepare more seriously a few months before leaving, my reasons for walking the Camino came into focus.

I begin to pay attention to my intention.

Surrender

Some people spend more time planning their vacations than the time they're on them. Sometimes that person is me. I've spent much of my life planning, organizing and trying to be in control of everything. I want to do the Camino because it will force me to let go of my need to control and allow me to just live day to day, step by step.

Sacrifice

I'm reaching a point in my life when I'd like to give more of myself for a greater good, and I hope to get some insight into how I can do that. In order to give more of myself, I'll need to be willing to sacrifice some of my personal comfort and security.

Storyline

It seems like the years are rushing by and I'm hardly noticing them. If all goes as planned, I'll finish the Camino on my 54th birthday. I'd like to invest those 54 years into my 55th and beyond, instead of just getting through another year. I'll have a lot of time to think about my life experiences, and the lessons learned along the way.

Suffering

This may sound like a strange reason to do something, but I've found that pushing myself beyond my comfort zone, especially physically, allows me to gain insights I wouldn't get otherwise. My athletic endeavors have included marathons, ultra-marathons and an ironman-distance triathlon, and I'm always up for a physical challenge. For me, *suffering is the price I pay to learn more about myself.*

Spiritual

The Camino is considered a pilgrimage. I don't have a specific religious mindset, so the definition of pilgrimage that works for me is "a physical journey with a spiritual intention." My hope is to return a better version of myself, Blaine 2.0. For instance, I want to be more patient, more tolerant of others and less judgmental. *I'm seeking to be transformed.*

During my preparation, I came across these thoughts on pilgrimage from Parker J. Palmer that resonate with me:

"Most of us arrive at a sense of self and vocation only after a long journey through alien lands. But this journey bears no resemblance to the trouble-free "travel packages" sold by the tourism industry. It is more akin to the ancient tradition of pilgrimage – a transformative journey to a sacred center, full of hardships, darkness, and peril.

In the tradition of the pilgrimage, those hardships are seen not as accidental but as integral to the journey itself. Treacherous terrain, bad weather, taking a fall, getting lost – challenges of that sort, largely beyond our control, can strip the ego of the illusion that it is in charge and make space for the true self to emerge.

If that happens, the pilgrim has a better chance to find the sacred center he or she seeks. Disabused of our illusions by much travel and travail, we awaken one day to find that the sacred center is here and now – in every moment of the journey, everywhere in the world around us, and deep within our own hearts."

Perhaps I'm ready to find my sacred center.

Today is my last full day in the USA. Tomorrow I fly to Paris and I feel a little stressed about what I'm about to do, plus there are a lot of loose ends to take care of before I leave, including work responsibilities and packing.

The timing of this trip couldn't be worse. Jacki (my amazing wife) and I just bought a home and have started several projects to make this house the way we want it. We wouldn't have planned the timing this way, but we found a home we really like and didn't want to let it slip away waiting until I get back from Spain. I'll now be gone for a month while Jacki deals with making decisions and working with our general contractor.

My intention to surrender is already manifesting, not only regarding our new house projects. I'm a big-time planner. I make

plans about plans, and I've spent many days coming up with a daily itinerary for this trip so that Jacki knows what town I'll get to each day and where I plan to stay. I'll stay in hostels, or *albergues*, most of the time and occasionally hotels when I'm in the larger cities. However, today, in the spirit of surrender, to have the freedom to stay where I want, when I want without being tied to my plan, I cancel my hotel reservations.

Oh God, what have I done?!

"All journeys have secret destinations of which the traveler is unaware." — Martin Buber

EXPECT THE UNEXPECTED

The *Camino Frances*, or the French Way, the most popular and well-supported route to Santiago is the one I'm taking, and most guidebooks suggest taking 35 days to complete it (including two rest days). My plan is to do it in only 26 days without any rest days.

Why would I make something much more difficult than what's recommended? The simple truth is I do not want to be away from home any longer than necessary. With my travel days to and from Spain I'll be gone for 31 days, which is the most I feel I can be away. I found sample itineraries on the Internet from people who've done it in 26 days. I figure if someone else has done it in that amount of time, so can I.

If you really want to do something, you'll find a way. If you don't, you'll find an excuse.

Yet how do I plan for something I've never done? I have no idea what the conditions will be like from day to day, how I'll feel, or what to expect. I don't know where or what I'll eat, or where I'll sleep each night. One thing is certain... my routine will not be what I'm used to.

I have 104 different items on my packing list, no exaggeration. Three pairs of socks count as one item; that means I have

well over 100 things to fit into my backpack. Everything I'll use to live away from home for a month I have to carry on my back, and I don't want the weight to exceed 25 pounds.

Some things I purchased for the trip I've chosen *not* to bring, like a compass with a temperature gauge, and a pedometer. I can gauge my direction based on the sun (unless it's cloudy, or dark) and it doesn't matter what the temperature is or how many steps I take, does it?

I need to stop measuring and quantifying everything.

The time to leave home has arrived, and I wish I was better prepared (that's the planner in me talking).

Jacki drops me off at the airport and we say goodbye. I've never been away from home for this long and even though she always supports the crazy things I do, I'm sure she's wondering if I'll change while I'm gone, and what that will mean for us. I hope that whatever changes in me will make me a better husband, but nothing is certain at this point. As she drives away, I'm sad to be leaving her, but excited about what lies ahead.

I travel a lot for work, and I never check my bag; I always want my luggage with me. My backpack would probably pass the carry-on restrictions, but my walking poles can't be taken on the plane, so I must drop my backpack off as checked baggage and hope we're reunited in Paris. Surrendering again my need for control does not come without a little bit of worry.

My 8-hour overnight flight will soon board and arrive in Paris tomorrow morning. As I wait at the gate, I realize I've left

my daily itinerary plan at home. I spent many hours figuring out how far I'd need to walk each day and which town I'd end up staying in each night. Even though my intention is to surrender, I'm not willing to leave without my plan! I text Jacki and ask her to take a picture of it and text it to me, so at least I'll have my itinerary on my phone. Jacki takes care of this for me, just like she does for so many things.

I miss her already.

"There are no foreign lands. It is the traveler only who is foreign." – Robert Louis Stevenson

FAVORABLE WINDS

The pilot announces we'll arrive in Paris an hour early due to "favorable winds." I hope this is a good omen for my trip. I do admit I'm slightly bummed to miss the ending of my movie. If you've seen *Avengers: Infinity War*, you know a lot happens at the end. I tell myself to get my head in the game. I'm not on a pilgrimage to watch movies!

My concern about being separated from my backpack is relieved when it finally arrives intact in baggage claim. Maybe it's the lack of sleep, but I find the Charles de Gaulle airport to be quite confusing. I also need to find an ATM and don't see one, so I wait in line to speak with someone who can direct me. I'm embarrassed as she points out the machine to my right with the large "ATM" on it!

I figure out how to find the right train to take into Paris to get to my hotel. (I didn't cancel *this* reservation, only the ones along the Camino.) Tomorrow I travel by train to the starting point of the Camino, the French town of Saint-Jean-Pied-de-Port.

My Paris hotel is a short walk from the train station and when I arrive, my room isn't ready yet. I didn't sleep on the plane, which means I've been up for over 24 hours, but I want to get adjusted to the local time (which is seven hours later than home) so I eat some snacks for energy and go exploring.

I've been to Paris a couple of times before but being here by myself isn't as much fun. I take the Metro to the Eiffel Tower and then to the Notre Dame Cathedral to say a few prayers for myself and my family. I find a park where the locals are playing football (soccer) and having picnics on the grass. I see a vendor selling freshly made crepes. I must have one! There's nothing like a Nutella crepe from a street vendor in Paris.

To ensure my phone is working I text Jacki and then call her. It's wonderful to hear her voice, and strange to be here without her.

I begin to transition to Camino-mode. Getting away from my normal routine is helping me to slow down and relax. After wandering for a few hours, I head back to my hotel and look for something to eat. Not wanting the fancy restaurants near the hotel, I stop in a grocery store for a pre-packaged sandwich, which isn't great but at least it's food. I need to get used to eating whatever I can find.

Back in my room, housekeeping provides several extra shampoos and conditioners to stash away for later, and I have no trouble getting to sleep.

"Not all those who wander are lost."
— J.R.R. Tolkien

READY OR NOT

Bonjour!

I'm up early this morning. It's a 30-minute walk in the dark to the train station, already bustling with people. It will take two trains and half a day to get to Saint-Jean-Pied-de-Port, which my guidebook describes as a medieval town with narrow streets nestled in the foothills of the Pyrenees.

I have an assigned seat on my first train, but I must leave my backpack at the end of the train car. It's interesting how protective you become over your possessions when you have so little.

The connection time to catch the second train is short, and in my rush to be ready to get off the train I leave my phone on my seat and have to go back for it. My use of technology will be limited this trip, of course, but not having my phone at all? I can't even imagine. I'll keep my phone in airplane mode during the day, so the battery doesn't drain down. Every night I plan to text my family to let them know where I've arrived for the night, and to send a few pictures from the day. I hope to talk to Jacki once a week.

Perhaps I'll check the weather forecast occasionally, and I have an app that shows the distance between the towns on the Camino and the hostel options at each location, but I have no intention of following the news, politics, the stock market, or sports. Other people may do the trek differently, but my thought is *why get away from it all if you're going to bring it all with you?*

There are three things I'm wearing that I don't intend to ever take off during my trip: my wedding ring, a dog tag with Jacki's phone number in case of an emergency, and my father's one-year AA medallion that I kept after his passing.

My dad had achieved twenty-one years of sobriety when he died at the age of sixty-two. The front of the medallion has the words "To Thine Own Self Be True" and the back has the serenity prayer, "God grant me the serenity to accept things I cannot change, courage to change things I can, and wisdom to know the difference." I thought these words are good reminders for my journey and a way to take my father with me.

With no assigned seats on the second train, we're packed in like sardines with backpacks and bicycles (some people do the Camino by bike). When we arrive in St. Jean, I let everyone walk ahead of me in order to take some pictures without people in them, when out of nowhere there's a jet flyover right over me! Strange. St. Jean is in a remote part of southern France. Is this a sign of some kind? Favorable winds? Godspeed? Just a pilot out training?

My jetlag from yesterday still affects me. I'm dealing with a headache and feel a little nauseous. I'm excited to get started tomorrow, but I'm also a bit nervous.

St. Jean is set up well to support all the pilgrims that start their Camino here, but I struggle with the language barrier and find it difficult to find food or places to eat as most restaurants close in the afternoon and don't reopen for dinner until 7 or 8pm... too late for me.

I booked a B&B to stay at tonight (okay, I didn't cancel this one either). On my way there I stop at the Pilgrim Welcome Center and am surprised by the camaraderie among people who don't know each other. There's a lot of excitement in the air and it appears that dozens, if not hundreds, of people will start their Camino tomorrow too.

My first "wildlife encounter" is a snake on the road that's no thicker than a pencil and faster than lightning. Instead of just admiring it, I get out my phone to take a picture. Of course it quickly slithers off into the grass. I need to remember that *sometimes it's better to capture an experience in my memory than with my technology.*

The B&B is run by Tim from England who is friendly and has the wit I'd expect from a Brit. My room is simple and comfortable; it has a huge shower but the smallest sink I've ever seen, not much bigger than a cereal bowl. I chose to stay at a B&B tonight because I want one more night of rest and solitude before staying in hostels. I'm not sure what to expect from communal sleeping and I'd like to start fresh on my first day walking the Camino.

I should be tired, but I have trouble falling sleep. Maybe I think too much about tomorrow and the days that lie ahead. Or maybe it's the church bells going off every hour that keep me awake. An owl hoots at midnight as if it's responding to the bells.

Whether I'm ready and rested or not, what I came here to do starts in just a few hours.

"Whatever you can do or dream you can; begin it. Boldness has genius, power and magic in it."
— Johann Wolfgang von Goethe

SPONTANEOUS PLANNING

Camino Day 1

St. Jean (France) to Roncesvalles (Spain)

16 miles

7 hours

7:45am–2:45pm

Today is my official start and it's also the International Day of Peace and close to the Fall Equinox. I like the idea of beginning my walk with peace and balance.

On this first day the Camino leaves France and crosses over the Pyrenees into Spain. The inclines are steep and long, and many people take two days to do it. I'm doing it in one. I had wanted to get an early start but I'm already behind schedule because I was enjoying the breakfast conversation at the B&B with Tim and a man from Vancouver, Canada.

As I leave town just after sunrise, I stop at a bakery to pick up two baguettes to eat throughout the day. I have trouble explaining to the woman at the counter that I'd like two separate bags so I can attach one to each side of my backpack. Fortunately, a Canadian from Nova Scotia who knows some French comes to my aid and I get the two bags I need. I meet up with him later and he tells me there's a hill coming up that will require us to "lean into it." That didn't begin to describe that hill, or any of the many others I would "lean into" today.

I've never hiked anything this difficult before, but the scenery keeps me mesmerized and I enjoy the many animals I see along the way: black-faced sheep with the occasional border collie, wild horses and hill ponies, pigs, Griffon vultures, and cows with big bells around their necks that clang when they move.

One of the customs that pilgrims follow is to say "Buen Camino" to everyone they come across on the trail. Loosely translated as "Good Journey," it's a simple yet effective way to express support to one another, and I find it especially helpful to give and receive an enthusiastic "Buen Camino!" when my body and mood are fading.

When there's a long stretch of trail without any towns or facilities, sometimes a local resident sets up a food truck or similar oasis providing nourishment and a place to rest and visit with other pilgrims. I stop at one of these for a Coke to drink with my baguette and sit down on the ground to look at my guidebook. Moments later I hear someone say, "You must speak English if you have *that* guidebook."

Liam from Ireland introduces himself. I tell him I'm from Chicago and he says that one of his all-time favorite people he's met on the Camino was from Chicago. I like this guy already. We talk for a few minutes and then he continues on while I stay to finish my snack.

Not long after that encounter, I catch up to Liam. We walk together and talk. Liam's upbeat, funny, and conversation with him is a joy. He spends ten days every year walking different parts of the Camino. He says it's the only time in his life that he's able to be completely spontaneous. Liam literally just drops himself somewhere on the Camino with no plan for how he'll spend the next ten days other than walking and meeting interesting people from all over the world.

I'm intrigued by the idea of not having a plan and tell him that I'd like to be able to do that. He warns me that it will take a lot of effort to give up planning, especially when planning is my usual way of doing things. I wonder if it's possible to be spontaneous *and* to have a plan at the same time, something like *spontaneous planning*. I like this idea and decide I'm going to strive to achieve it while I'm on the Camino. Liam stops to talk to some people he met earlier, so we say goodbye for now and I keep walking.

After literally walking above the clouds, there's a steep descent into the town of Roncesvalles, my destination for the night. The trail splits into two, a more difficult but more direct path and an easier but longer one. I take the harder one. Too bad I didn't spend more time at the Pilgrim Welcome Center in St. Jean. Apparently, they warned people not to take the more direct route, not just because it's harder but also dangerous due to loose rock on the trail and the decline is *very* steep. By the time I figure out I've made the wrong choice, it's too late to go back. I persevere and am rewarded at the bottom with a walk through a beautiful forest that the other way doesn't have.

There's only one hostel in Roncesvalles and it can accommodate almost 200 people. The B&B in St. Jean had suggested I make a reservation here, and it's a good thing I did. Pilgrims arriving just after me without reservations were turned away because by then it was full; they had to take a taxi to the next town to find a place to sleep.

This hostel is newer, and the bunk beds are set up to sleep groups of four people in what feels like a cubicle. My "group" consists of a woman from southern California, a man from Italy who speaks no English, and an older man from Dublin who's walked the Camino several times.

Even though the walk was quite strenuous today, I feel good, and I'm grateful that I can even attempt this feat. Thank you, body, for not breaking down on the side of the trail!

After showering I eat dinner at a nearby restaurant and sit at a table with some retired women from Florida who are walking the Camino together. Whenever I tell people I plan to do the entire thing in 26 days, I get puzzled looks as if to ask if that's even possible. I have my own silent doubts. Based on the distance I covered this first day, I'm already behind what I need to average daily to meet my goal.

After dinner I walk into a church just in time to attend a special pilgrim's Mass and blessing. I don't usually understand what's happening in a Mass and I especially don't understand tonight because it's in Spanish, but from what I can tell there are two Bishops in attendance, which is a big deal and not the norm. At the end they call out all the countries represented and ask the pilgrims to come to the front of the church for a special blessing. Even though I don't understand all the words, I'm moved to tears.

Walking back to the hostel a woman asks me where I'm from. The United States, I reply. She waves her hand around her face and tells me I have a "Portuguese face." Then with a "Buen Camino," she walks off. I'm not sure if that was a compliment or not, but I take it as one!

Back in my bunk-bed cubicle, the man from Dublin warns me about women who travel the Camino alone. "They're looking for a husband," he tells me. "Beware of seduction!" I don't think this will be a problem, and I've got my wedding ring on in case there's any question about my availability.

Hostels have strict rules about lights out and quiet at 10pm. They also kick you out early in the morning in order to prepare for the next wave of pilgrims arriving later in the day. I've never slept in the same room with dozens of other people. I hope it goes well.

"A good traveler has no fixed plans and is not intent on arriving." – Lao Tzu

AMBITION GONE WILD

Camino Day 2

Roncesvalles to Pamplona

27 miles

12 hours

7:00am–7:00pm

The symphony of sound I heard last night was unreal. The snoring was constant. One person would stop, and another would start. Then they'd snore together, one higher pitched than the other, or one going up the music scale and the other coming down. The snoring, coughing and farting seemed to go on all night. At one point I just laughed at the absurdity of it all and did my best to relax and not get stressed about not sleeping.

At breakfast, my bunkmate from Dublin brings me a cup of coffee and says, "I assume you take it black because that's how you drink it in America." What? I don't. In fact, I like a little coffee in my cream and sugar! All along the Camino, black coffee is referred to as *Cafe Americano.*

It's still dark as I head out and I have trouble seeing the ground in front of me. I toy with the idea of going farther than my plan calls for today. Based on how the towns are spread apart, if I go the distance that's on my plan, I'm still not averaging what

I need to each day. I'm feeling good and it seems like now is the time to push farther and gain some time in case I have problems later. However, the next town past my planned destination is Pamplona, which for most people would be a two day walk from where I'm starting. I'll see how the day progresses and decide later.

The morning starts out foggy and cool with plenty of shade under tree-lined paths, but later I walk out in the open blazing sun with the temperature around 90 degrees. Yesterday most of the walking surface was on roads or relatively smooth trails. Today the trails have become more technical with lots of ups and downs and sharp rocks coming out of the ground that are beating up my feet. I only brought one pair of shoes, which are trail running shoes, and I begin to question if I need something with a harder bottom, so I don't feel the rocks as much.

Throughout the day people ask me how far I'm going and when I mention Pamplona the reaction is usually the same - a look of disbelief and that I've lost my mind. When I arrive at the town I had originally planned to stay in, I rest a bit while having a snack and I feel good enough to keep going. Pamplona here I come! As I cross the bridge leading out of town, Liam is just arriving. We say a quick hello and goodbye, as it's probably the last time I'll see him. Friendships are easy to form on the Camino, but they're brief.

As the afternoon wears on, my enthusiasm fades. There are long stretches where I'm alone and can't see any other pilgrims ahead of or behind me. I'm tired and blisters start to form on my feet. Not a good situation, but I made the decision to go to Pamplona and I must live with it. At one point I become disoriented and my mental state starts to deteriorate. I'm not sure I could have spelled my name if I was asked to. I can't tell where I am on my map even though I'm following the Camino trail markers and I have no idea how much farther it is to Pamplona. I eventually get so exasperated I look up at the sky and scream. Aaaah!!

I. Have. Had. It.

It's only the second day and I've made a huge mistake! The only thing I know to do is turn back and retrace my steps until I find a place to stay for the night, and it kills me to think about going backwards.

Earlier in the day I had stopped in a small village to see what kind of food was at the grocery store. As I left the village, a man who had just arrived there stopped me and asked if the grocery store had "sun cream." Ah, a Brit looking for some suntan lotion. We struck up a conversation and he (Fleming) asked where I was headed to today and I said, "Pamplona." Unlike the other reactions I'd gotten, Fleming appeared to be intrigued with the idea that it's possible to go that far in one day. A few minutes later two sisters from Australia arrived and we all started chatting, but I needed to keep moving so I wished them "Buen Camino" and continued walking.

Now just as I turn around in absolute frustration, I see three people coming towards me… it's Fleming and the Aussie sisters!

I don't believe they would have been there if I hadn't had that chance encounter with them earlier in the day and planted the seed of possibility in their minds that it was possible to go all the way to Pamplona. And now they were there to rescue me! They had a GPS app that was literally giving them turn-by-turn directions to Pamplona. They knew exactly how far it was and encouraged me to follow them there. I didn't think I had it in me, but they helped me "find another gear" and we walked together to Pamplona. I try to be independent and not need anything from anyone, but sometimes *we need each other.*

Grateful and exhausted, I make it to Pamplona. My feet are in bad shape and I choose to stay in a hotel and not a hostel. I need to fix my feet and sleep in a comfortable bed without dozens of people snoring around me. I also want to do some laundry. Unfortunately, it's Saturday night, and by the time I arrive the laundromat is closed and won't reopen until Monday. I do the best I can to wash my clothes in the bathtub and dry them with a hair dryer.

I'm in pretty good spirits but worried about my feet. Blisters can be a game-changer and could potentially end my trip prematurely. I need to be smarter and make better decisions from now on. My overconfidence in how well things went yesterday cost me dearly today.

I learn the importance of bringing balance to ambition.

Back at home, a spontaneous family reunion has formed at our house with relatives from five states coming in to see Jacki's parents, my in-laws. It started with her brother coming to visit and took on a life of its own as more and more people made the trip. Many of these people haven't seen each other in over ten years. This doesn't just happen. I think there was some divine intervention that brought everyone together. I would have liked to have been there to see everybody, but I'm okay where I am... I made it to Pamplona! The daily itinerary I gave to Jacki is now worthless, and *I'm ahead of schedule.*

As I go to sleep, I smile thinking about the festivities at home that are just getting started.

"Tourists don't know where they've been,
travelers don't know where they are going."
— Paul Theroux

SAME PATH, DIFFERENT WAYS

Camino Day 3

Pamplona to Cirauqui

20 miles

8 hours

8:30am–4:30pm

It's said that the Camino has three distinct sections: Physical, Mental and Spiritual. I don't know if it's the same for everyone, but these first few days for me feel like the physical part, as I endure difficult terrain, relentless sun, and heat.

I'm able to sleep in this morning because I'm at a hotel, so I don't get started as early as I have the last two days. Pamplona is the largest city along the Camino (population of 200,000) and it takes a while to get back out into the countryside. Once I do, I pass two women who are dressed in traditional pilgrim attire from long ago and they're traveling with a mule (they're walking, and the mule is carrying their gear). The mule doesn't seem motivated to do the Camino and they continually prod it forward.

It's still early in the day, but so far, I feel balanced physically and emotionally, which is a relief after yesterday's meltdown.

I've noticed that many people walking the Camino don't have large backpacks like I have. In talking with them I learn that you can hire someone to take your belongings ahead to wherever you're staying that night, and all you need to carry is whatever you need to get through the day. That seems more like a vacation than a pilgrimage to me, but for some people it may be the only way they can walk the Camino.

Everyone travels the Camino in their own way, just like we all travel through life differently. I'm struck by the realization that *it's not necessary to pass judgment on the decisions that other people make.* We all live our own lives and make our own choices. I knew this before coming to Spain, but I now understand it and feel it at a level that's much deeper than I ever have before.

The walking is difficult today. My blisters continue to bother me, and my right hip has started to hurt. I've thrown out some of the packaged food I brought from home to lighten my load… anything to make things a little easier on my body. Carrying twenty-five pounds doesn't affect my upper body as much as I thought it would, but it's adding a lot of stress to my lower body.

The pilgrims on the Camino are generally friendly and on their best behavior. I've observed only one person being angry, and immediately after he spoke harshly to his travel companion, he walked right into a thorny bush and ended up with blood running down his arm!

I've witnessed many acts of kindness along the trail. On a particularly difficult descent one man helped another hiker down the hill so he wouldn't fall. Another woman who walked with a limp and seemed to be having a lot of trouble putting one foot in front of the other was given a walking pole from another pilgrim so she could support herself better. That spirit of camaraderie that I felt at the Welcome Center in St. Jean exists all along the Camino.

I stay in Cirauqui, a medieval hilltop village. After checking into the hostel, I take what may be the best shower I've ever had. The water running down my body feels good and I cry tears of joy, mixed with laughter. I'm sure someone watching this scene would think I've lost my mind. I'm not usually an emotive person, but the Camino is peeling away my outer layers and I'm feeling and expressing emotions more intensely.

The albergue is comfortable and our host prepares a wonderful dinner. She speaks several languages and when I ask her if she has walked the Camino herself, she says no, but that she's going to close the albergue in a month, then she can finally experience the Camino as a pilgrim. My dinner companions are from Ireland, Denmark, France and Italy (the Italian speaks almost no English, so we communicate with gestures).

We talk about how we're holding up and the woman from Ireland offers to work on my blisters, but I feel uncomfortable accepting help (my independent nature doesn't always serve me well). We discuss how old we are and one of the young women from Denmark thinks I couldn't be older than 40... she's now my favorite person at the table! I'm impressed at how many young women are traveling the Camino on their own, and no, I don't believe most of them are looking for a husband, despite the warning I was given in Roncesvalles.

When it's time for bed, I can't sleep. The pain in my legs and hips keeps me awake, and at times I can feel an energy racing through my legs, almost as if I'm feeling the healing that takes place during the night. It doesn't help that the open window by my bed is across from the village church, and the bells go off every fifteen minutes.

All. Night. Long.

"The real voyage of discovery consists not in seeking new landscapes, but in having new eyes."
— Marcel Proust

LET'S ALL GET ALONG

Camino Day 4

Cirauqui to Los Arcos

23 miles

9 hours

6:45am–3:45pm

I appreciate being around people from all over the world, always interested to learn about other cultures and hear different perspectives. Many of the people I come across are curious about what's happening in America, especially with our politics (I walked the Camino two years into the Donald Trump presidency). Apparently, our politics are in the daily news all over the world, and many of the changes and challenges we're experiencing in the U.S. are also happening in other countries. Overall, people seem to have great admiration for our country and our people, and they're able to separate our citizens from our politics. I wish we could do the same. *Separating the person from their ideology isn't easy, but it's necessary if we're going to coexist. Even when we disagree, we need to listen to each other.*

It's dark when I leave Cirauqui and I use my headlamp for the first time. It's still morning when I arrive in Estella, a town with a population of 14,000 people. My limited Spanish makes it difficult to communicate as well as I'd like to, and getting through the larger towns is challenging because the markings for the Camino are much harder to find among all the other signs, lights, signals, etc.

As I focus on not getting lost, two women approach me from the opposite direction, and one of them asks, "Do you speak English?" Finally, I have an opportunity to use my native language to help someone! I reply that I do speak English, and she proceeds to tell me that she and her friend are Jehovah's Witnesses and asks if I'd be interested in taking one of their brochures.

"Sure," I reply with a huge grin on my face. What are the odds of getting stopped by an English-speaking Jehovah's Witness in Spain? I walk on and glance at the title of the brochure: "Will suffering ever end?" I laugh and think it's an appropriate topic for what I'm doing!

After leaving Estella I enter a long, wooded section of the trail and realize I should have gotten some food while I was in the city. Just then I spot a banana that someone left on a large rock for whoever needs it. That would be me! "The Camino provides" is a popular expression among the pilgrims and it came true for me today. I'll buy some fruit at my next opportunity to leave on the trail for someone else.

My left foot is a mess with more blisters forming, and my heel is getting tender. The best way I can describe my foot pain is to imagine that the bottom of your foot is sunburned. That's what every step feels like. The pain slows me down and changes the way I walk, which causes my leg joints and back to ache because I'm not walking properly.

I also find myself alone on the trail more and more, sometimes not seeing anyone else for a few hours. I start to talk out loud to myself... a lot.

It's another warm day but the weather is changing. It's windy and supposed to get down into the 30's tonight. Yikes, that's going to feel quite cold after the heat of the last few days. To save space and weight, I didn't bring a sleeping bag. I only have a sleeping bag liner that's designed to trap your body heat to keep you warm. Fortunately, the hostels have blankets I can use if I'm cold.

When I reach the town of Los Arcos, I choose which hostel to stay at, and get the last bed they have... a top bunk that's on the 3rd floor... not the greatest situation given the condition of my feet, but I'm happy to have secured a bed for the night. I go to a grocery store to find some dinner and observe an Italian woman squeezing some fruit that specifically has a sign in front of it with the words, "Don't touch the fruit." The store owner confronts her, and the woman says she can't buy fruit without checking it out first. Then she complains about the prices, at which point the owner goes on a tirade in Spanish, and I can only imagine what the words are. Note to self: Don't be confrontational with the locals, especially when you don't know the language well.

The ups and downs on the Camino are continuous. Not just the terrain, but emotionally. My first day went great. The second day I had a meltdown. Day three was balanced. Today has been another long, difficult day… I had to push hard, but I didn't come off the rails!

Sleeping continues to be a challenge. I am exhausted at the end of the day, but I lie down to sleep and can only close my eyes and rest. Someone suggested that the endorphins my body is producing by walking several hours a day could be changing my biochemistry, and maybe that's why I lie awake at night. Regardless of the reason, I'm okay with whatever amount of sleep I get. *It is what it is.*

"Travel is fatal to prejudice, bigotry and narrow-mindedness." – Mark Twain

HEEDING ADVICE

Camino Day 5

Los Arcos to Logrono

18 miles

7.5 hours

7:30am–3:00pm

A group of young men in the bunk beds surrounding mine were noisy up until 10pm last night, but then quickly quieted down when it was lights out. And for the first time, I slept well in a hostel! Woohoo!

It's the coldest morning yet at 40 degrees and I wear my jacket, hat and gloves. Many of us are heading out early and we see the moon setting in front of us and the sun rising behind us.

Here are some of the interesting things I've observed along the Camino:

- Sometimes the Camino is on roadways where you must be mindful of cars. Maybe it's because there are hundreds of people walking these roads every day, but it seems like the drivers would just as soon run over you. They don't slow down for pedestrians and will speed by just inches away from you.

- The dogs in Spain are aloof. You could try to get their attention by waving a steak around and they'd ignore you. The exception are the dogs who live in the albergues who are more like pets. We tend to treat our pets as members of our family in the U.S. I don't think that's the case in Spain. Or perhaps it's just that animals in rural areas are often used more for utility than companionship.

- The trail markers along the Camino vary from place to place, but the most common is simply a yellow arrow, often painted on the road, a building, or a large rock. The markers can be easy to miss, especially when you're walking through a town. The general advice is that if you haven't seen a marker or any other pilgrims for a while, you're probably not on the Camino. Another common expression is that if you're not going uphill, you're going the wrong way!

- Farmers don't live on their farms; they live in the nearby villages. When you walk through farm country you don't see any buildings or residences, and in the towns, you'll often see tractors parked in front of homes next to the family car.

- Spaniards take their siesta time seriously. Stores and restaurants will close by 1 or 2pm during the week and won't reopen until several hours later. They also close early on Saturday and are closed on Sunday. I had to keep this in mind when planning where I would stop for food. If you enter a town or village during siesta time it feels like a ghost town. The larger cities might have a few more places that stay open, but not many.

- Dinner is often not available at restaurants until 8pm. You can order drinks earlier, but not food. This doesn't work well for me and I often buy food at a grocery store.

- When you're walking in town and someone is approaching from the opposite direction, they don't make any eye contact, but when they get alongside you, they'll utter a greeting just as they pass you. I'm used to greeting people as they approach but the locals don't seem comfortable with this.

- Stop signs in Spain read STOP. I was expecting something else.

- Especially in the larger cities, the locals smell great. Men, women, young, old, you name it... fragrance sales must be booming. Me, on the other hand, I don't think I smell badly, but in the late afternoons in the rural areas I have a lot of flies harassing me, and that's not a good sign given where flies like to spend their time.

I'm beginning to realize *I need to listen to other people more and be willing to take their advice*, especially when they know more about something than I do. My attempts at taking care of my feet aren't working, so I take some of the advice I've been given and stop at a *farmacia* (pharmacy) to purchase Compeed blister cushions, talcum powder to put in my socks and petroleum jelly to put on my feet in the morning. Hopefully this will help.

I walk so slowly because of my foot pain that it's taking me a long time to cover the distance I need to each day, which means I'm hesitant to take breaks. I'm not sure this is a good idea. I notice that other people stop several times a day, often taking time to have a meal at a restaurant, and they seem to be holding up better than I am. I'm going to start taking more rest breaks, even if they're short.

Most people don't walk as far as I do each day because they're taking the recommended 35 days to get to Santiago. Walking 15 miles a day is much more doable than the 21 that I'm averaging. Those last several miles at the end of the day are when it's hot and are the most difficult miles to get through. Oh well, unless I want to take a bus or train for part of the Camino, I need to average almost 20 miles a day to get to the end in the 26 days I've given myself to do this.

My destination today is Logrono, and even though the distance isn't that far, it's a struggle for me. I've elected to stay at a hotel again. It's almost a mile off the Camino and it's adding some distance to my walk both today and tomorrow morning. On the plus side, I get to do my laundry at a legitimate laundromat for the first time. I wear my clothing at least 2-3 times before washing, and they need to be laundered. As much as I'd like to wash every article I have, I need to walk a few blocks to the laundromat, and I don't want to get arrested for public nudity.

Imagine an American walking around in long running bottoms that look like jazz pants, with flip flops on his feet, wearing a red long sleeve shirt on a hot day, and he's not wearing any underwear. That would be me. To make matters worse, the laundromat is hot inside and I can't stand being in there while my clothes are washing and drying, so I wander around the neighborhood looking like this. Good thing I'll never see any of these people again!

The hotel has upgraded me to a lovely room and I'm able to soak my weary bones and muscles in the bathtub and do my nightly foot surgery before settling in for the night. I'm not interested in watching television, but I'm able to listen to music through the TV and I find a station that plays a lot of American hits from the 80's. Perfect.

"Travel makes one modest. You see what a tiny place you occupy in the world." — Gustave Flaubert

A NOISE LIKE NO OTHER

Camino Day 6

Logrono to Azofra

22 miles

9 hours

6:15am–3:15pm

I start early today, and I can walk normally! This is exciting and gives me an extra bounce in my step.

A strange thing happens to me this morning. I'm alone on the trail for much of the morning and at one point I look behind me and see several men walking quickly who are coming up on me. I cross the main road heading into a town and when I look back again, they're gone! I can't see any other place they could have gone to, but there's no sign of them anywhere. I'm either seeing spirits on the Camino or I'm seeing things that aren't there. Either way *there's some woo-woo going on here.*

It was another "push" day, but after nine hours I didn't have any new blisters! It was windy today with a steady 15-20mph "favorable" wind (mostly at my back). The high temperature was about 80 degrees and the wind made the afternoon feel comfortable. I experimented with taking more breaks, which made for a longer day but may have made it easier for me to cover the distance that I did.

The albergue I choose to stay at is a new building with a unique configuration - you share a small room with only one other person. There's just enough room for two beds and two small closets, and the bathroom is at the end of the hall. Two of us arrive within a few minutes of each other and we're put in a room together.

My "roomie" is from South Korea and speaks little English, but when he does talk, he does it enthusiastically! He's traveling with more technology than I own at home, including a recording device that is videotaping every step of his walk across Spain. He must place the camera on his head, and it records all day long, capturing everything he's seeing. He also has a heavy battery and charger to ensure he captures each step from St. Jean to Santiago. I give him credit for carrying so much gear, and I think he's nuts (in a non-judgmental way, of course!).

Europeans, especially Spaniards, are the most common nationalities on the Camino. I've also met a lot of Canadians and Australians, and surprisingly, there are a lot of people from South Korea. I made the mistake of referring to them as being from South Korea, but many of them want to be referred to simply as Koreans because they don't acknowledge North Korea. I try to find out why so many people from Korea are doing the Camino, and one explanation I'm given is that it has become a significant thing to put on their resume. Competition for good jobs and promotions is intense there and walking the Camino has become a status symbol.

Many of the pilgrims at the albergue end up at the same restaurant for dinner, and I sit with a young woman from Taiwan. Most of the peregrinos doing the Camino are one of three types: students, retirees, or people between jobs. Not many pilgrims are gainfully employed like I am, probably because taking a month or more off from work isn't an option for most people. Many of the younger "millennials" have recently left jobs they didn't like, and they're not worried about finding another job when they return home.

My dinner partner from Taiwan, who speaks English well, tells me her name is "Jessica." Jessica is her American name that she chose in first grade when she started learning English. This is a common Taiwanese custom and this name often stays with them throughout their lives because pronouncing their given names would be too difficult for most people.

As I get ready for bed, I notice my roommate is applying several nasal strips to his nose (I didn't know you could have more than one on at a time). As soon as we turn off the lights, I discover why he does this. I've never heard snoring like this before. Full-bodied and completely through every inhale and exhale. There's no way I can sleep through this; I wander through the albergue in the dark trying to find another place to sleep.

Everything is locked up for the night and there isn't anyone there to help me. I find what looks like a metal park bench near a window, but it's uncomfortable, and I can appreciate why a homeless person might prefer to sleep on the ground. Wait a minute, that gives me an idea. I return to my room and carry my mattress down the hall, lay it on the floor and try to sleep. I can still hear the snoring from down the hall but at least it's muffled a bit. Unfortunately, I've placed my mattress by the bathroom, and a lot of people walk by me when they get up during the night to pee. I spend much of the night worried that someone will trip on the mattress in the dark and fall on top of me.

I only sleep a few hours. Again.

"If you want the rainbow, you've gotta put up with the rain." — Dolly Parton

THERE ARE
NO COINCIDENCES

Camino Day 7

Azofra to Viloria de Rioja

18 miles

8 hours

6:30am–2:30pm

If I played the lottery, today would be the day to buy a ticket.

After returning my mattress to my room, I'm one of the first people to leave the albergue this morning. It is a little tricky finding my way out of town and back to the trail when it's dark, especially when no one else is out walking yet.

Occasionally there are some "alternate" paths along the Camino; they're the roads less taken, so to speak, and may be longer than the official Camino route. The benefit of taking these is there are fewer people on the trail and the paths are often in a more natural setting. Even though I can't afford to add more time or mileage to my journey, I occasionally take these alternate paths when I feel up to it. They require that I pay more attention than usual because these paths are often not marked well.

It takes almost four hours to reach Santo Domingo, the first town I come to that's large enough to have some breakfast options. The cafes are busy, and even though the owners/employees are working as fast as they can, it can take a while to get served. I stop at a couple of places that are too busy for my liking and end up at the grocery store to buy some lunch meat and milk, which I eat while sitting on a park bench outside of a church.

Today is another balanced day in terms of time and effort. I'm dealing with a new problem, which is the result of being in the sun too much. Skin is peeling off my nose and forehead, and I'm getting a sun rash on my arms (something I'm prone to when I spend too much time in the sun). To limit my sun exposure, I may have to wear long sleeves even though it's warm. I haven't shaved since leaving France and I've decided to grow a "Camino beard," if it doesn't drive me crazy and irritate my skin.

My emotions continue to wash over me throughout the day. My children have only seen me cry a few times ever, and yet I'm crying several times a day on the Camino. I never know what will bring on the tears... a beautiful sunrise, pain, missing home, feeling grateful... you name it, it could be anything. One thing is certain, *this is by far the hardest physical challenge I've ever attempted.* If I knew how hard this would be, I may not have resolved to do it. Of course, one of the reasons it's this hard is that I'm walking farther each day than is recommended and I'm not taking any rest days.

The hostel I want to stay at is in the village of Viloria de Rioja, which has a population of 28. Yes, you read that correctly. 28. I hope they all like each other! The albergue is called *Refugio Acacio & Orietta*, and as soon as I walk in, I know I've made a good choice. It feels like I've entered someone's living room. There's incense burning and several comfy chairs and couches to relax on. The place can accommodate up to ten people but there are only four of us here, all American men from the Midwest. We're told it's the only time they've had only Americans stay there in the 20 years they've been in business.

Before leaving the U.S., I'd told a colleague about the Camino, and coincidently, her father was also going to be walking it around the same time. She said he would start before me and take a slower pace, so he'd finish after me. This means at some point I'd pass him, and she hoped we might meet each other somewhere along the way. She described him as "an old white guy with a mustache from Ohio named Dave." It's not like we wear name tags, and you can't believe how many old white guys with a mustache I've seen along the way.

After getting settled in at the hostel, I introduce myself to John and Arch, friends who are traveling together, when the other American approaches me and asks, "Is your last name Rada?" I respond, "Have we met before?" He tells me his name is Dave, and his daughter had told him about me. Unbelievable! What are the chances that we'd meet somewhere on the Camino, and even more incredible that we're staying at the same albergue. *There must be a reason we've been brought together.* Dave and I spend some time getting to know each other and we agree to keep in touch as we make our way to Santiago.

Our hosts, Acacio and Orietta (he's from Brazil and I think she's from Italy) prepare an amazing meal and join us for dinner and conversation. They met on the Camino and have walked it several times. Acacio wanted to live somewhere along the route and they eventually opened an albergue, devoting their lives to helping other pilgrims.

The conversation becomes personal as we share why each of us are walking the Camino. We're all hoping to grow spiritually, which leads to a common expression, *"The Camino will give you what you need, not what you're looking for."*

Orietta adds some additional thoughts by saying that "The Camino will interfere." In other words, the Camino will do its work on you no matter what, and it may not even happen until afterwards. She also believes in the expression, "la mente miente," or "the mind lies." *We can't always trust what's in our head.*

As much as we're enjoying the conversation, we all need our rest, so it's off to bed. It's the second time I'll sleep well at a hostel.

This has been the most spiritually enriching day on the Camino thus far. I am truly blessed to be doing this.

"Listen with your heart, you will understand."
— Grandmother Willow, Pocahontas (movie)

A MONSTER DAY

Camino Day 8

Viloria de Rioja to Atapuerca

24 miles

10 hours

7:30am–5:30pm

Unlike most hostels that want you to leave no later than 8am so they can prepare for the next wave of pilgrims, the rule at Refugio Acacio & Orietta is that you *cannot* leave before 7:30am because they want you to rest and sleep in.

Orietta is up early to prepare a simple breakfast for us. Even though we've only known each other since yesterday afternoon, we all feel like family. As we get ready to leave, John and Arch sing a blessing song to Orietta that has us all in tears as we hug each other and head out.

It will be another monster day for me, although not as difficult as previous long days. The "monster" theme starts when I get my backpack ready for the day. A large spider is on the edge of the opening to my backpack and it could easily wind up inside, which would mean I'd have to empty the pack completely to find it. I'm able to brush it off with my hand... although I didn't see where it went once it was on the floor!

The next "monster" I encounter is another snake on the trail. It's coiled up right in front of me and doesn't move as I get closer. As I get right up to it, I realize it's dead and I nudge it gently with my walking pole to make sure. Coming across dead animals (usually small ones) on the trail has happened more than you would think.

A few hours later I come to a gas station and stop to use the bathroom. Whenever I use the bathroom in a public facility, I feel I should purchase something there, and I have a craving for some chocolate milk. They don't have any, but they have something just as good that I haven't seen since I've been in Spain... Monster energy drink. I frequently drink these at home and am thrilled to find one, but it doesn't have a resealable lid, and I'll have to carry it with me on the trail until I finish it.

As I walk with my Monster drink in one hand and my two walking poles in the other, I notice someone walking towards me. He has an athletic build and is dressed in what looks like biking gear, but he doesn't have a bike. We say hello as he passes by quickly, and then moments later I hear "Where did you get that?" I turn around and he asks where I got the Monster drink; I tell him at a gas station a couple of miles away.

We spend some time talking and I discover he's a famous athlete, Jason Lester, an endurance runner, the author of *Running on Faith*, and the 2009 ESPY Award winner for Best Male Athlete with a Disability. He's American, lives in Hawaii during the winter, and spends the rest of the year running all over the world. He's running the Camino in the opposite direction, from Santiago to St. Jean, and this is just the start of his run through Europe. We give each other some heartfelt encouragement and get back to walking/running. You never know what brings people together on the Camino. Today it was a Monster energy drink!

Later this afternoon there's a "monster" climb I'll hike in the heat, and unfortunately, more blisters start to form. I stop to do some blister repair before they get worse. I've been experimenting with taking ibuprofen at different times to see what works best. Today I take some in the middle of the day, which I haven't done before, and I think it makes a difference in how I feel as the day wears on.

At the peak of today's climb an oasis has been set up by a local resident. All the food and drink are free of charge, she only asks for a donation. The atmosphere is jovial, with people greeting one another and enjoying the break from the trail. I sit down for a bit and talk with a young couple from Australia.

By the time I get to my destination for the day, the town of Atapuerca, I don't feel like eating and don't even want to take a shower. I just need to sit down and do as little as possible. I call Jacki for the first time since I started walking the Camino. Hearing her voice makes me feel much better! Even though she has a lot going on at home, she doesn't bring any of that up because she wants me to be able to focus on the task at hand and not be distracted by anything else. I can't express in words how amazing she is, always looking out for other people, especially me!

Atapuerca has been declared a UNESCO World Heritage site because our prehistoric ancestors lived there, with the earliest human remains (Homo Antecessor) in Europe dating back at least 1.2 million years. It's fascinating to think about how long people have walked on the same ground I'm walking on.

My extra effort has put me one day ahead of schedule, but my body is paying the price. It was probably a mistake not to eat dinner because I need fuel to heal, and even the ibuprofen isn't relieving my pain. It was also a mistake to skip taking a shower because I feel hot and sticky. I used some *Combat Wipes* to clean myself, and now I smell like a freshly washed baby's bottom.

It's another night of difficult sleep. *My mantra is becoming "Accept and Adapt."*

"If you don't stop, you can't be stopped."
— Jason Lester

REST AND REFLECT

Camino Day 9

Atapuerca to Burgos

12 miles

5 hours

7:30am-12:30pm

My shortest day of walking on the Camino, but certainly not an easy day.

It's still dark when I begin and almost immediately there's a long climb on rocky ground. I'm irritated that I'm starting my day with an all-out effort, and the relentless hills and rough terrain continue to batter my feet. So much for *accept and adapt*.

Several physical irritants are on my mind today: Pain has been a constant companion along the Camino, especially my feet; my sun rash is bothersome; and I'm losing patience with the afternoon flies that won't leave me alone. As I approach Burgos and walk near the airport, there's a nasty stench in the air and the flies in that area are particularly bad.

Past the airport, there's a beautiful biking/walking path that leads into Burgos. It's Saturday morning and hundreds of locals are enjoying the outdoors along the path. I eventually enter the city and make my way toward my hotel. As I come to a church, I go in. I often stop at the churches that I encounter on the way and go in for a few minutes when they're open. In this one a Mass is taking place and I stand in the back just in time for the sign of peace... one of my favorite parts of Mass!

After checking in to my hotel, I immediately take a shower. Then, I'm off to find a laundromat, and I'm dressed more appropriately than the last time! The washing machine automatically dispenses its own detergent, and I hope I won't mind the scent and won't have a skin reaction to something I'm not used to. I spend the afternoon strolling around Burgos, and I haven't felt this good this late in the day the entire trip.

I choose to behave like a tourist today, which includes having some gelato and a real dinner at a real restaurant. I order vegetable paella, which is a Spanish dish of rice, spices, and (usually) seafood cooked and served in a large shallow pan. Yum!

I use the extra time to rest and reflect. I've enjoyed my time in Spain, but I miss Jacki and wish we were here together. My limited Spanish isn't enough to communicate effectively; if I return someday, I'll need to learn more Spanish to have real conversations with the local people.

After nine days on the Camino, I feel like I'm transitioning from the "physical" portion to the "mental" section. Tomorrow I reach the region known as the *Meseta*. I've been warned that this section is hard on your mind because the terrain is miles and miles of flatter landscapes without the undulating trail and the spectacular views I've grown accustomed to seeing each day.

I'm comfortable being alone with my thoughts and look forward to the change in scenery, especially the flatter ground.

"Almost everything will work again if you unplug it for a few minutes, including you."
— Anne Lamott

IT'S NOT THE PLACE, IT'S THE PEOPLE

Camino Day 10

Burgos to Castrojeriz

23 miles

9 hours

6:30am–3:30pm

Finding my way out of Burgos is a challenge, and I get lost for the first time on the Camino. I join a group of (mostly) Americans who are leaving the city at the same time I am. Rather than following my own instincts and directions, I follow this group who walk confidently and seem to know where they are going… until they don't. Their approach is to fire before aiming, so they walk until they no longer see any trail markers, and then they ask the locals how to get back on the right path. We eventually find our way out of the city, but I should have left them back when I thought they were going the wrong way. I continue to walk and talk with them for a while, but their pace is faster than mine, and I start to get some muscle pains in my groin and don't want to keep pushing my pace faster than I should. They gradually get ahead of me without us saying goodbye.

Today I enter the Meseta. I bake in the sun all day as there's little shade, and I wear long pants, even though it's hot, because my sun rash is also on my legs now.

I've been getting plenty of *Vitamin N*, or time in Nature. I've become more attuned to the natural environment that I'm spending many hours in each day, and my heightened senses are picking up slight shifts in the weather and the movement of the animals around me. I'm beginning to dislike the time I spend in larger cities; they're loud and busy compared to the quiet and solitude of the rural areas.

I could go farther today but decide to stop on the outskirts of Castrojeriz. I'm interested in staying in a unique albergue… the ruins of the 12th century Monastery of San Anton, a portion of which has been stabilized in order to make it safe for people to be there. The monastery was founded in 1146 under the patronage of King Alfonso VII, and it was the main Preceptory of the Antonian monks in Spain. This order was dedicated to the care of pilgrims and to cure those who suffered from the "Fire of San Anton," a disease that spread during the Middle Ages.

The albergue consists of two rooms that are separated by a half wall, one for sleeping that accommodates about a dozen people and a kitchen/eating area. There's no electricity, which means there's no hot water. Guess who won't be taking a shower tonight? And there's no Wi-Fi (pronounced wee-fee, which is kind of fun to say!); fortunately, I anticipated this and texted home earlier in the day.

We have a communal dinner before it gets dark, and our volunteer hosts ask that we introduce ourselves and describe in one word what we're feeling on our Camino. I say "grateful." The group includes a young couple from Pennsylvania, a father and son from Austria (the father was biking slowly, and the son was walking quickly), two young women from Canada, a couple from Poland, and young men from Israel and Belgium. Our two hosts are from Poland and Mexico, and they tell us it is the last night the albergue would be open for the season due to the nights becoming cold and their limited facilities (no heat).

I initially wanted to stay here because I thought there would be something special about staying in ruins that are over 1,000 years old. But there is nothing special about the place; *what made it special was the people who were there.* Having casual conversations and sharing a meal with such a diverse group of people warms my heart.

The young man from Israel has walked the Camino several times, including some of the other routes, and when I ask him why he keeps coming back, he says it's because of the people he meets along the way. Amen, brother.

"We must understand each other to trust each other."
— Celeste Headlee

MOVING THE GOAL

Camino Day 11

Castrojeriz to Poblacion de Campos

20 miles

8 hours

7:30am–3:30pm

Breakfast by candlelight is magical. I don't want to leave the company of these people, but we each have a journey to continue… we say our goodbyes with hugs and head out. It's a very simple life on the Camino. You get up and start walking. Later in the day you stop walking. Then you get up the next day and repeat the process. Along the way you meet people, eat, shower, wash clothing, and sleep. I wonder what it will be like the first morning after I finish when I don't have to walk anywhere.

It's dark as I set out and I hear owls hooting in the distance. The only other sound is the click-click-click of my walking poles hitting the road. I have many thoughts during the day that I don't want to forget, so I start using the voice recorder on my phone to capture them.

My guidebook tells me there will be a "strenuous climb," a "massive hill" coming up. It hasn't referred to any of the other climbs in this way, and I can only imagine what I'm in for. For the sake of comparison, the maximum grade allowed on federal highways in the U.S. is 6-7%. The climb today is a 12% grade going up and an 18% grade going down. A decline that steep is extremely hard on your knees, and I see someone walking down backwards (with assistance from another person) to take the pressure off their knees.

It's October 1st and Nature says it's time to change seasons. There's a strong wind from the north all day, probably about 15-20mph, that hits me from the side and makes it hard to stay upright, especially with my backpack providing a lot of wind resistance. Sometimes I can become agitated when I'm in the wind for long periods, but it doesn't bother me at all today. It's cloudy for much of the day and it's the first time I keep my jacket on until the afternoon.

There's a song by Mumford & Sons, *I Will Wait*, that replays in my head all day. I don't know the meaning of all the lyrics, but they're comforting to me and seem to be urging me on.

It's my second day on the Meseta and I'm enjoying this "mental" section of the Camino. I don't agree with the warnings I'd been given that this portion is boring and that the landscape isn't pretty. It's different from what I saw during my first nine days, but I find it beautiful in its own way. I don't see much water along the Camino, but each body of water, be it a river, stream, or pond, looks amazing and I have a strong desire to jump in.

One of the largest towns I walk through today is Fromista. As I leave town, I notice I haven't seen another pilgrim or any trail markers for some time and begin to wonder if I'm going the wrong way. I'm walking on a sidewalk in a residential area when I spot a young child in their front yard. Should I attempt to ask if I'm still on the Camino? I don't have to because as I approach, he looks up at me and says, "Buen Camino." I must be going the right way!

I could have gone farther again today but I want to stay at a hostel that has a unique setup. The beds are in little pods with a light and a couple of shelves, and a curtain you can close for privacy. At dinner I meet people from England, Brazil, Spain, Germany, and Korea. After finishing dinner, I continue a conversation with the German couple and the man from England (who has done portions of the Camino many times).

Just as I planted a seed of possibility in Fleming's mind that he could go all the way to Pamplona on my second day, the Brit plants a seed of possibility in my mind tonight… if I continue at my current pace, I could go past Santiago and walk all the way to the coastal town of Fisterra… the "end of the world." I've heard that some people do this but didn't think it was possible for me because it takes another two to three days beyond Santiago to get there.

I wonder…

"Wonder is the beginning of wisdom." – Socrates

A-HOLES

Camino Day 12

Poblacion de Campos to San Nicolas del Real Camino

31 miles

12 hours

5:45am–5:45pm

Today is my earliest start yet, which means I'll walk in darkness for at least a couple of hours. The main route goes along a highway for several miles, but I'm taking an alternate path that's in a more natural setting and follows a river. I could easily miss some trail markers in the dark, but if I keep the river to my left, I should be okay.

I like walking in the dark, not able to see that far in front of me and only hearing the crunching of gravel under my shoes, but when I hear something unusual or unexpected, it's a bit unnerving. I'm aware that if anything were to happen to me in such a remote area, it wouldn't be a good situation. I'm already worrying my family just by doing the Camino, and adding additional risk seems foolish (perhaps selfish?) on my part. At the same time, I've taken these kinds of risks most of my life, and I almost can't help myself.

I periodically look behind me to see if any pilgrims or vehicles are on this gravel road with me, and I notice a light in the distance that's moving in such a way that I think it's another pilgrim who's also taking this alternate path. I keep checking behind me and the light appears to be getting closer; I imagine he/she must be walking faster than I am, which isn't a surprise. And then the light disappears!

There is no other road or path they could have gone down other than the road I'm on, and it would be foolish to navigate this terrain without a light. Why is the light no longer behind me? I never get an answer to this question, and once it starts to become light, I never see anyone behind me. A few days ago, I saw people who disappeared behind me and now I've seen a light that was coming towards me from behind that suddenly went out. I have no explanation for these events.

Eventually the alternate path connects to the main Camino route, which runs along the highway. There aren't any markers indicating which way I'm supposed to turn. My instinct is to turn right, so that's what I do. Shortly after that I'm approached by two pilgrims coming from the other direction who are walking with a lot of purpose and seem to know what they're doing. Am I going the wrong way? Every morning the direction of the sunrise has been behind my right shoulder, which is where it is today. I'm still not sure I'm going the right way until I begin to see other pilgrims walking in the same direction I'm going.

There's a long stretch of ten miles coming up that has no support along the way... no towns, water, or bathrooms, so I stop in the city of Carrion de los Condes to stock up on food and water. I stop in a café to get my usual items (Coke, bread, and maybe something sweet), and when the proprietor tells me the total, it seems too much. I've purchased these items for several days and know how much they generally cost (often there are no prices on merchandise in the cafes), and I have this feeling in the pit of my stomach that I'm being overcharged. I'm not about to get into an argument in Spanish so I pay the man and go on my way. I figure if he's taking advantage of pilgrims walking the Camino, that's his problem, and he'll have to live with the consequences. I'm able to move on and let it go, but it's still sitting in the back of my mind as I leave town.

At about the halfway point of the ten miles of nothingness, a local resident has set up an oasis where people can sit down and purchase some food and drink. I've walked several miles in the sun on lonely, straight roads surrounded by fields that have already been harvested, and I can use a break. I sit down at a picnic table and take out the Coke I purchased earlier, wondering if I'll buy anything to eat while I'm here. Within a couple of minutes, the owner comes up to me and asks what I want to purchase. I tell him I'm just drinking my Coke for now and that I'll let him know if I'm interested in anything else. Keep in mind these conversations don't go as smoothly as I describe them. My limited Spanish and their limited English make for difficult communication, with lots of gestures and awkward pauses as we try to understand one another.

He then tells me I must leave if I'm not going to buy anything. What!? I can't believe it! I put my hand on my heart and ask him, "Am I not welcome here?" He shrugs in agreement and says it wouldn't be appropriate to go to a bar and bring your own drink. I feel a rush of emotions. I'm angry and hurt and am wondering if this is just a tiny bit of what it feels like to be a member of a group that isn't welcome or wanted somewhere. Trying to take the high road, I put on my pack and walk out, saying, "Adios Amigo. Peace."

But I'm not feeling any peace. I'm pissed off. Adrenaline is racing through my body and I walk at a fast pace driving my walking poles into the ground with each step. I've been wronged! The injustice of it all! I know what I'll do… I'll notify the writers of the Camino guidebooks and tell them they should put a note in their books that warn people who might stop at this oasis. Don't stop unless you're going to buy something! This guy doesn't care about being of service to pilgrims, he's just interested in money! My mind races on…

And then I start to cry.

But I'm not crying for the reason I'd expect. I'm not emotional because of what was done *to* me. *I'm upset because of the way I'm responding.* Is this really who I am? The first thing I think to do when someone is unpleasant to me is to strike back? This isn't who I thought I was.

He didn't need to change. I did. And he was there to show me this. The Camino keeps giving, and I'm grateful. But it took my anger and tears to realize this.

Maybe it was the energy of my emotions, or the flat terrain and wind at my back, or the afternoon flies I was trying to get away from, but it ends up being an extremely long day. Over 30 miles and 12 hours of walking bring me to my stop for the night. I'm glad I'm sharing a room with only one other person. He's from Germany, and when I tell him about my experience at the oasis, he says, "What an asshole." I laugh, wondering if this is an expression used in Germany too.

And he's right. I ran across a couple of asses today. People who didn't treat me the way I want to be treated. So what? Life happens. Get over yourself. And then it hits me...

How we handle adversity can either define or destroy us.

Speaking of asses, can we talk about butts for a minute? Because my butt crack may need medical attention. Maybe this doesn't happen to people with small butts, but mine is a little larger, and my butt cheeks rub against each other when I walk. Thirty-one miles of walking is a lot of rubbing together, and a lot of friction, a lot of heat. It feels like my butt crack is raw. Of course I can't see down there, so I go to the bathroom and close the door that doesn't lock, hoping no one will walk in. I take off my shoes, pants and underwear, and put one of my feet up on the sink with my backside facing the mirror while I turn my head around to try to see what's going on back there. I don't think it's supposed to be that red! I apply some of the talcum pow-der I bought for my feet in the hope it will reduce the friction. Thankfully no one walks in on this scene and I'm off to have dinner with my fellow pilgrims - after putting my clothes back on and washing my hands of course.

Our dinner table has three Koreans, two Frenchmen, and my German roommate. The dinner portions are huge, and I eat everything that's put in front of me. I burned a lot of calories today and need to replenish them.

Tomorrow might be another long day. I hope my butt holds up.

"An eye for an eye only ends up leaving the whole world blind." – Mahatma Gandhi

LAUGHTER IS
GOOD MEDICINE

Camino Day 13

San Nicholas del Real Camino to Reliegos

24 miles

10 hours

6:45am–4:45pm

Pilgrims attach a scallop shell to their backpack, which identifies them as a peregrino on the Camino. When I packed for the trip, I had two shells from Florida that I considered using. I'm traveling with one and I left the other one at home with Jacki as a way for us to stay connected. I don't think it would be a good sign if my shell breaks along the way, and so far, it's holding up well.

Today's finish will mark the half-way point, based on the number of days I've allotted to get to Santiago, and I'm still at least one day ahead of schedule. It's nice to know I have some cushion in case I need it later.

The village of San Nicholas del Real is small, but I have a hard time finding the trail once I leave the albergue. There are a few of us out at this early hour and we're all a bit confused as to which way to go. As I continue to look for the trail markers, a small group of pilgrims confidently head off together in the opposite direction; I eventually follow them hoping they're on the right path. They are.

After such a long day yesterday, my physical and emotional energy is drained. I'm just not into it today, and I stop at a café for some breakfast. My usual breakfast consists of café con leche and tortilla (not what you think, it's a Spanish omelet) with bread. The café (they're called "bars" in Spain) appears to have just opened and is playing upbeat music that lifts my mood. I notice how much care the bar owner takes in preparing my food, even seasoning the bread in a way I haven't seen before. There's a woman mopping the floor and a small cat attacks the mop, only to slide across the wet tile floor. This comical scene repeats itself several times… the cat runs at the mop, slides across the wet floor, and runs away to prepare for the next attack. The woman, the bar owner, and I all start laughing at the cat's antics and my mood has completely changed.

When I return to my normal life, *maybe I should start my day with something that makes me laugh*, which probably won't be the news. With my mood lifted, I notice the birds chirping as I leave the café with renewed energy.

I want to reach the city of Leon tomorrow, which means I have a difficult choice to make today. Based on how the towns are spaced apart, I can follow yesterday's grueling walk with another long day today and a shorter day tomorrow. Or, I can do a shorter day today followed by a long day tomorrow. If my body can handle it, I'd prefer to do another long day today, this way I'll have time to relax in Leon.

In the town of Sahagun, the Camino de Madrid (another route to Santiago) joins the Camino Frances and suddenly the trail is more crowded. I notice many more Spaniards on the Camino now and they appear to be having a great time… lots of enthusiastic conversation, stopping for beers along the way, and even taking taxis to finish their day when they're tired of walking. As I've said before, there are as many ways to do the Camino as there are people doing it.

The hostel I stay in is run by a man named Pedro. If you've seen the movie, *The Way*, he reminds me a lot of the character named Ramon. Pedro isn't eccentric like Ramon is, but he's a real character, especially as he explains the rules and procedures that he expects me to follow while staying there.

Joining me at the communal dinner table are folks from Canada, Denmark, and New Zealand. One of the Canadians shares a story about having to leave her travel companion behind a couple of days ago, because of an injury that prevented her friend from continuing. On the day the injured person was told by a doctor she couldn't continue, she woke up to find her scallop shell broken in half. She was exactly at the half-way point of the Camino. There's a lot of woo-woo stuff that happens out here.

This being my half-way day, I thought I'd do a body scan to see how I'm holding up:

Lower Body

Blisters

Hips (pain during the day and ache at night)

Foot trauma (soles are sore, and I'll likely lose a toenail)

Upper Body

Sun Rash

Beard (irritating my skin)

Lower back (tightening up)

So far, *the Camino is what I expected, it isn't what I expected, and it's more than I expected.*

And in case you're wondering, my butt crack is doing much better.

"You are that which you are seeking."
— St. Francis of Assisi

SUFFERING IS OPTIONAL

Camino Day 14

Reliegos to Leon

16 miles

7 hours

6:30am–1:30pm

Taking off my shoes at the end of each day is like unwrapping a present… you never know what you'll find. My blister problem is getting ridiculous, and the pain has become so intense that stepping on the smallest stone causes me to wince in pain.

Today was supposed to be an easy day getting to Leon, if it weren't for the pain. I'm desperate to find relief and choose to "cheat" just a little bit. The Camino often follows alongside a roadway and walking on the road is easier on my feet than walking on the rocky trail. I must stay alert though, because the Camino can turn away from the road at any time and I'd need to get back on the trail, which may not be easy due to things like ditches and fences. I also must be mindful of traffic, which doesn't like sharing the road with pilgrims. Walking on the road this morning in the dark is especially dangerous, and I'm distracted by the sounds of horses moving around on the other side of the roadway fencing. I have a flashlight and a headlamp and do my best to make sure cars can see me.

There's a long, steep descent into Leon and by the time I enter the city my feet are killing me. Just as I feel I can't take any more pain, a cat walks over to greet me and flops down on my feet as if to say, "You don't have to walk right now, just pet me." I miss our cat Gryffin, and there have been many feral cats to interact with on the Camino.

Two of my original intentions in making this pilgrimage were *surrender* and *suffering*, and I've decided to surrender *to* my suffering. *I may be in a lot of pain, but suffering is optional.* Other people have dealt with a lot of pain, and so can I. In fact, many people have dealt with a lot worse than what I'm dealing with. Of course, I'd prefer to be able to walk normally and not be in discomfort, but perhaps this is exactly what I'm supposed to experience on my Camino. Once again, I realize this isn't about me and *I need to get over myself.*

I stay at a hotel in Leon, and after getting settled I head out to find a laundromat. I'm the only one doing laundry there until a woman comes in. She's confused about using the machines and asks me for help by trying to speak Spanish. She's relieved when I tell her I'm an American and I explain how to use the machines. She and her husband are from England and are walking the Camino together, and I learn that all three of us have birthdays this month. Another interesting coincidence.

There's a shopping mall across the street from my hotel and I'm curious to see what a mall is like in Spain. It's more like a huge department store with many levels, each one devoted to a different type of merchandise. As I get off the escalator on one of the top floors, the first thing I see is a wall of shoes, and I decide it's time to buy a different pair of shoes. As a runner, I know this could be a big mistake, perhaps one of the dumbest things ever done on the Camino. You don't put on shoes you've never worn and that aren't broken in during the middle of a marathon. The number of shoes displayed on the walls is staggering, and my feet literally walk me over to a specific pair. I ask if they have my size and they do! I try them on, and my feet immediately feel better. Sold!

Leon is the last big city I'll be in until Santiago, and I need to find a farmacia to stock up on *ibuprofeno*. I've been using it more than I thought I would, and I'll run out of it soon. I talk to the pharmacist and find out I can get a higher dosage (600mg) than you can get in the U.S. Forty tablets cost just over $2. Unbelievable. I wish medications at home were this affordable.

As I reflect on my journey, this feels like the last "mental" day of my Camino, and I wonder, how do I achieve the peace of mind I've felt here when I return home? Here's what came to me: peace of mind isn't based on the absence of conflict, or on having only pleasing circumstances, or even the absence of thought itself. *Peace of mind is available the moment you realize it's the natural order of things. It's available in every moment.* I need to remember this.

Jacki and I talk on the phone for over an hour tonight. It has been a great day in Leon… new shoes, stronger ibuprofen, finding some peace of mind, and talking to the love of my life. Life is good.

"Knowing yourself is the beginning of all wisdom."
— Aristotle

TEMPTATION

Camino Day 15

Leon to Hospital de Orbigo

22 miles

8.5 hours

7:30am–4:00pm

I've tied my original shoes to the bottom of my backpack and with each step they hit me in the butt, prodding me along like the mule I saw outside of Pamplona.

Every day has been physically challenging but entering the Meseta on Day 10 shifted my focus to the "mental" part of the Camino. The Mesata landscape allowed me to spend several hours each day alone with my thoughts, not having to concentrate on my foot placement or looking for trail markers. It was kind of like being on cruise control when the road is straight and there's little traffic on the road with you. The "mental" portion lasted only five days for me. I've processed my thoughts about the things I came here to think about and am now entering the "spiritual" part of my Camino, and I look forward to this part the most. It has already been a spiritual experience for me, but now my intention will be more focused in this area.

My new shoes feel good on my feet, and while I may get some new blisters because the shoes aren't broken in, the rocky ground I'm walking on isn't as painful as it has been for the past two weeks.

I stop at a café this morning after walking for a couple of hours. As I sit outside looking at my guidebook, a young woman arrives who gets the attention of everyone there. She's traveling alone and looks like she could be a model. She has a natural beauty that turns the head of every man at the café; she's perfectly tanned and has just a small amount of perspiration without being sweaty. She orders hot tea and some type of pastry and eats daintily while reading her guidebook. I notice how mesmerized the other pilgrims are and remember the warning I got on my first night about women traveling alone on the Camino, "They're looking for a husband. Beware of seduction!" She doesn't seem to be paying attention to anyone else. Could that be part of her plan?

Oh, for crying out loud, Blaine, you need to get back on the trail and stop thinking about this! Which is exactly what I do.

Several hours later, when I'm walking along the side of a road, I come across another snake. It's dead and looks like it may have gotten cooked on the hot blacktop. What is with all the snakes?! Then I start thinking about what spiritual lesson might be in store for me today. Snakes have long been associated with evil and temptation. But I like snakes! Wait a minute... what about the young woman I saw earlier at the café? Seductress +

Snake = Temptation! What in the world does temptation have to do with anything?

As I meditate on this word while continuing to walk, I come to my own definition of what temptation is and how I should deal with it in my life. *Temptation is an optional detour that takes you off your path. The best way to handle it is to move it aside and keep walking. Stay on your path.* The challenge of course, is that I have the power of choice. As I continue to think about this all afternoon, I have the desire to recommit myself to be a better husband to Jacki. I've never been tempted to be unfaithful to her, but my attention is often distracted by the many detours I take (like this trip to Spain) and I need to be more discerning and focused on staying on *our* path.

The hostel I've selected, *Albergue Verde*, is almost a mile off the main Camino, but hopefully will be worth the extra walking. I'm greeted with a glass of ice water as soon as I enter, and the owner takes time to get to know me before we discuss the accommodations and cost. It has a hippie vibe with some dogs and kittens running about. It's the first time a dog has come up to me wanting attention since I've been in Spain, and one of the kittens climbs up my chest and snuggles under my chin. I'm in heaven.

I spend some time outside enjoying the animals and catching up on my notes when I hear a commotion, like people who haven't seen each other in a long time greeting each other with excitement. I look to see who it might be and lo and behold, it's the young woman from the café this morning! I learn that she's from Holland and she's reuniting with another young woman she met earlier on her trip. And no, I don't think she's looking for a husband on the Camino!

The hostel offers a yoga class that I pass on. I wouldn't take a yoga class at home, so it's not a good idea to take one now. While most of the pilgrims are in the class, I'm treated to guitar music and singing from one of the volunteers, while other volunteers prepare an incredible organic, vegan dinner.

I meet some people from Norway and Australia, and my dinner tablemates are three women from Denmark and a woman from New York City. When I tell them about everything that's going on at home, they tell me I have a "super wife" and they hope I realize how lucky I am. I've known that from the day I said, "I do!"

The owner of the albergue, Viktor, is from Sweden and has an inspiring story. He grew up with abusive parents who were drug addicts; in fact, his father died when Viktor was eight, and he was relieved he was gone! Viktor eventually turned to drugs himself and came close to dying from an overdose several times before finding help from an organization called *Here For You*. After four years of being drug-free, he started a project called Every Step Counts (www.everystepcounts.se) to raise money and awareness for *Here For You*. He decided to walk the Camino and started from Sweden! Along the way, he filmed his experiences and his thoughts about life, which ultimately became a documentary film called *Every Step Counts*.

It's Friday night and Viktor breaks his own "lights out at 10pm" rule so he can show us his documentary. Yay, it's movie night! I learn in the film that when he walked from Noorkoping, Sweden to Fisterra, Spain he stopped at an albergue that felt truly special to him; in fact, he didn't want to leave. It turns out this is the albergue he fell in love with, and he eventually moved to Spain to purchase it and spend his life here. Watching him press on beyond Santiago to the coastal town of Fisterra has me wondering for the second time if it's possible for me to do the same. Time will tell.

From a troubled childhood to a teenager with a death wish, Viktor now devotes his life to caring for peregrinos making their pilgrimage to Santiago. He can't let us go to bed without taking a few minutes to explain how to find our way back to the trail tomorrow morning in the dark. Many of the volunteers who help him are pilgrims who stopped here for a night and chose to stay longer, from a few days to several weeks. If I didn't have such a tight schedule to maintain, I might have stayed longer too.

"To reach Fisterra in Spain is my final goal.
Exactly how I will get there, I do not know."
— Viktor Jinnevang

ALONE WITH GOD

Camino Day 16

Hospital de Orbigo to Manjarin

30 miles

11.5 hours

6:45am–6:15pm

I didn't hear any snoring last night and I slept well! I'm the first one up and out the door after making some toast and coffee. Last night the volunteers set a table with everything the pilgrims would need for breakfast.

Viktor had recommended we take an alternate path today that avoided walking along the highway. It's remote, and even though it's dark, I turn off my headlamp, trusting I won't fall on the ground that I can't see in front of me. I hear what I think are coyotes until I realize that dogs are howling in the dark. I'm a little nervous that they may be loose and would come at me, but I have two walking poles and I can make a lot of noise myself if I have too!

As I pass through a small village in the dark, I come across a man sitting on a chair in his garage who has prepared some food to pass out to the pilgrims coming by. I'm probably the first person he's seen this morning and I have the best pick from the platter of food he presents to me. I thank him and go a little further into the village, noticing a building foundation that seems to be an abandoned construction project. It looks like a house was being built and I walk along the foundation walls to determine how big the structure was supposed to be. As best as I can measure by my footsteps it's approximately 20 feet wide by 40 feet deep. That's 800 square feet along the outside perimeter, much smaller than the typical house in the U.S.

As the sun begins to rise and I can see the ground in front of me, I notice two acorns by my feet that are lying next to each other in such a way that they look like a heart, and I think of Jacki. I begin to understand why some people walk the Camino more than once. Even though I have no intention of doing this again, I feel the magic that keeps people coming back for more. I had the same intention after running my first marathon, and I ended up doing more of them, and even longer distances, so I guess you never know what the future holds.

The first large town I come to today is Astorga (population of 12,000). I'm having trouble following the trail, when a man walking down the street motions for me to follow him. I don't understand what he's telling me, but I think he's showing me a shortcut that avoided a difficult crossing of a busy road. The shortcut involved walking across railroad tracks (not at a crossing), and it's the second time I've had to do this on the Camino to find my way back to the main trail.

It's Saturday, and even though it's cold and windy today, I come across several groups of locals who walk parts of the trail for recreation. At one point a woman says to me, "Que Tal?" and I can't even remember enough Spanish to realize she's asking me "How are you?" Sometimes I feel like a real dufus out here!

In another small village I find a store that has something I've been searching for… chocolate milk! It's a large container, at least a quart or more, but I buy it anyway even though it's going to add a lot of weight and bulk to my backpack. I rationalize that it will provide enough nourishment for the rest of the day in case I have trouble finding food later.

A thought came to me today. I usually think of my journey through life as being focused on going forward, but *the road isn't just in front of me. Looking back can be incredibly instructive. Looking side to side takes the focus off myself. Looking above inspires me and looking below reminds me of my connection to the Earth and to those who have come before me*, especially my relatives. Their DNA, influence, and my memories of them continue to guide me.

By late afternoon the weather is deteriorating. I'm climbing into the mountains and it looks like a storm is on top of the mountains and heading towards me. I have a decision to make; I can stop now in a village with plenty of hostels to choose from, or I can press on and take my chances in the next town that only has one hostel, but according to my app, can accommodate 39 people. Continuing in this weather could be a big mistake, but there's an important reason I want to do just that.

In between this village and the hostel with 39 beds is the highest point on the Camino, known as Cruz de Ferro (Iron Cross). This simple iron cross on top of a weathered pole stands atop a pile of rocks and has become one of the most significant symbols on the Camino. The tradition is for pilgrims to bring a stone with them to this point (the stone can be from home or found along the way), and to leave the stone as a symbol of something they are releasing, something they don't want to have to carry with them any longer. If I wait until tomorrow to reach Cruz de Ferro, there will be a lot of other people there, and based on what I've already seen along the Camino, there will be a lot of picture taking and commotion.

Maybe I'm selfish, but I want to be alone at this place. I brought a stone from home and want this to be a spiritual moment. If I continue walking into the storm, I'm almost guaranteed to be there by myself, but the trail conditions could become difficult. I know what my family would prefer I do, but I didn't come here to play it safe; I keep walking.

The weather continues to deteriorate with mist, spotty rain and a lot of wind. I should probably put my rain poncho on to keep my backpack dry, but the wind would only blow it around and I don't want it to get caught on anything as I walk. The trail becomes rockier and the rain is making the rocks hazardous to walk on. I notice there's a road that seems to be following the

Camino and elect to walk on it, which is a great idea until I lose sight of the trail and have no idea if the road will get me where I want to go. The weather is getting worse by the minute; even the cows in the fields are miserable and are wailing like Chewbacca in *Star Wars*.

I start to question my decision to walk on the road now that I can't see the trail, but I know that Cruz de Ferro is a local landmark and I trust that the road will take me there. It's the only road I've seen and I'm still going up, so I must be going in the right direction. The mist has turned to rain and I'm getting wet.

It takes a lot more walking than I expected, but I arrive at Cruz de Ferro, and I have the place to myself. As bad as the weather is, it's still beautiful and I'm overcome with emotion. It's steadily getting colder as I take out my stone and climb the pile of rocks already there, searching for the perfect place to leave mine. Before setting it down, I say the following:

God, thank you for keeping me safe and getting me here. I'm leaving this stone as a symbol of what I'd like to release from my life. I release my need to be in control, and my need to understand every-thing. These traits may have served me in the past, but I don't want to carry the weight of them any longer. Thank you.

I feel lighter already, and I need to keep moving. Knowing I'd be in a remote area, I've already sent a text to my family and told them they wouldn't hear from me again until tomorrow. The hostel is about thirty minutes away and I'll be soaked by the time

I get there. As I press on, I see footprints in the wet soil, which tells me a couple of other people are just ahead of me.

Arriving at the hostel I am physically drained but spiritually energized and am greeted outside by the owner. I tell him I need a bed for the night, and he says they're full. What?! How is it possible that 39 other people have stopped here for the night? In the middle of nowhere and under these conditions?

I ask how far the next town is and he says seven kilometers. That will take me at least two hours, and the weather and trail conditions will continue to get worse. I resign myself to the reality of the situation and ask if I can dry myself off and rest a moment before continuing. His eyes tell me he feels sorry for me, and after a moment he thinks of something he can offer… a mattress on the floor. That'll work! I'm happy to sleep on a mattress on the floor.

This hostel doesn't sleep 39 people, it sleeps nine, and I'm number ten. All ten of us will sleep in a one-room stone hut from the 12th century that doesn't have any electricity or running water. The nine people who arrived before me get to sleep on wooden platforms that are up off the ground and run along the walls; I will sleep on the only floor space that's also needed to enter and exit the hut. I'm wet, have nowhere to put my belongings, and everyone is staring at me as I attempt to set up camp on a mattress on the floor.

There's a wood-burning stove on the side of the mattress where I plan to put my head, and the other end of the mattress is in front of the door. The spaces between the door and the door jamb are large enough to let small animals in even when the door is closed. I attempt to change into dry clothes in front of everyone while standing on my mattress. I've gone from an emotional high to an emotional low and proceed to drink the entire container of chocolate milk I bought earlier!

The stove isn't putting out much heat and I can't get warm, even wearing several layers of clothing. For dinner, we all walk in the rain to another building where the meal is served, and I finally warm up after eating several bowls of soup. Many of the people who arrived before me have formed friendships with each other even though no one traveled here together. I try to keep track of where people are from as we introduce ourselves and I believe there are people from Italy, Denmark, Ireland, Israel, Brazil, Hungary, and Korea.

After dinner we return to our hut and find that the stove has been re-stocked with wood and is putting out so much heat that I can't stand to be near it, and I start removing my layers of clothing. With no electricity, we light some candles for light. With no running water, I'm obviously not taking a shower, and I'm not even going to brush my teeth because the water I have with me is too important for tomorrow for me to use it to rinse my mouth tonight. What about going to the bathroom? There's a pit toilet across the road. I'm not sure what a pit toilet is, and I discover it's exactly what it sounds like. After navigating uneven, wet, rocky ground and crossing a road, there's a little wooden shack with a door that reminds me of an outhouse. Once inside, you need a flashlight to see, and all you need to see is a hole in what looks like a wooden pallet that *sits on the ground.* Wow, this is gross.

Things get worse.

After we all turn in for the night (leaving the candles burning in case someone needs to get up to go to the "bathroom"), the young man from Italy and the young woman from Denmark decide to do their part to increase international relations. They are literally close enough to me that I can reach up and touch them, and I get to listen to the sounds of lovemaking for what seems like an eternity. I've heard that hook-ups like this aren't uncommon on the Camino, but I didn't think I'd be within arm's length of one! I would tell them to "get a room," but we're all in the only room there is.

You wouldn't believe how many people get up during the night to use the pit toilet. The door creaks when it's moved and doesn't close properly, and I have to get up several times to latch it to keep the cold air from rushing over me all night.

To make matters worse, as the wood burns in the stove, it gets colder and colder, and by midnight there isn't any heat. Another night of very little sleep.

"The place God calls you to is the place where your deep gladness and the world's deep hunger meet."
— Frederick Buechner

ALL ROADS
LEAD SOMEWHERE

Camino Day 17

Manjarin to Ponferrada

14 miles

5 hours

8:30am-1:30pm

I wake up to the sound of singing monks… a recording that's played over loudspeakers to indicate breakfast will be served in fifteen minutes.

The storm has passed and it's a beautiful, but cold, morning. At breakfast I sit next to the female half of last night's hook-up. I wonder if she's aware of everything I heard. A few minutes later the other half walks in and they exchange glances.

Today will be a much shorter day for me and I plan on staying in a hotel tonight. I need to do some laundry, but being Sunday, I'll have to use the bathtub in my hotel room since the laundromats will be closed.

I'm tired of walking on rocks and seek out smoother surfaces, even walking on roads that may be longer than the official trail. The descents, even on the roadways, can be quite long and steep, and it feels like my toes are getting crushed into the front of my shoes.

Sometimes I'm not sure the road I'm walking on is going where I want to go, but *all roads lead somewhere, even when you feel like you're going nowhere.* Each step moves me forward, hopefully closer to my goal of reaching Santiago. In fact, I'm now *two days ahead of schedule* and I ponder what walking another 50 miles past Santiago to Fisterra would be like.

My phone storage is running low, so I'll have a project to work on tonight… *delete what's unnecessary to create more space.* That sounds like a good project for life itself!

I was looking forward to staying in Ponferrada, a town that has my last name in it, but Sundays aren't good days to explore a city. Stores and restaurants are closed, and even though I walk a few miles around town I can't find anything to eat. Fortunately, I have enough food in my backpack to fuel me until tomorrow. My hotel room has a balcony and I'm able to hang my laundry over the railing to dry… it's windy, and hopefully it doesn't blow away.

It's been about ten days since I saw my new friend Dave from Ohio. I send him an email to see how he's doing and find out he's been dealing with some illness and has had to take the train for 77 miles of his Camino to get back on schedule. He's disappointed of course, and I tell him *it takes courage to acknowledge your limits and to do what you need to do for yourself.* I don't always take my own advice.

"Be a lamp, or a lifeboat, or a ladder.
Help someone's soul heal. Walk out of your home
like a shepherd."
— Rumi

MY HEART IS OPENING

Camino Day 18

Ponferrada to Las Herrerias

27 miles

11 hours

6:30am–5:30pm

I stop at a café for some café con leche this morning and guess who I see there? The young Dane who had the hookup with the young Italian in the freezing one-room hut the night before last! I find out she's only 19 (yikes) and she isn't traveling with the Italian… it was truly a one-night stand.

Before leaving the café, another pilgrim sings a song and plays her recorder for the woman working there. I walk with her a short while later. From her singing, I would have guessed she is French but find out she's Swiss. I ask her about the song she sang in the café and she tells me it's called "Ultreia," which comes from Latin, loosely translated as "onward and upward." It seems fitting to me because I think of the Camino as both physical (onward) and spiritual (upward). The song was written down in the *Codex Calixtinus*, the first Camino de Santiago guide, dating back to the 12th Century.

She tries teaching me the lyrics in French... yeah, that's not happening. Later I look up the English translation:

Every morning we take the Camino,

Every morning we go farther,

Day after day the route calls us,

It's the voice of (Santiago de) Compostela!

Onward! Onward! And upward!

God assist us!

Way of earth and way of faith,

Ancient road of Europe,

The Milky Way of Charlemagne,

It's the path of all the Santiago pilgrims!

And over there at the end of the continent,

Santiago waits for us,

His smile always fixed

On the sun that dies at Fisterra.

I would have enjoyed walking some more with her, but we aren't walking at the same pace and I continue ahead of her.

Today is the first day I have no idea how far I'll go or where I'll end up. I'm reminded of my ironman-distance triathlon experience; after swimming 2.4 miles and biking 112 miles, I still had to run a marathon (26.2 miles), but I knew I could walk the entire marathon and still reach the finish line by the race cutoff time of 17 hours. Now that I'm two days ahead of my original schedule, I don't have to worry about how far to go each day, because I know I'll reach Santiago by the 26th day even if I slow down a bit (barring any unforeseen injury or illness of course).

Later in the afternoon I come across three women who ask, almost in unison, "Where are you headed to today?" I answer, "Wherever I stop." One of them responds with, "That's the spirit!"

I've done it, I thought. I've gotten to the point where I'm not planning out every detail of my day. Liam the Irishman would be proud! I certainly feel a little proud.

I come to a spot on the trail where I have a choice between two routes; a shorter one with a lot of hills on rocky terrain, or a longer one that is smoother and flatter. Given that I'm still developing new blisters I choose the longer but smoother one. I pass by the turnoff for the shorter option and keep walking, confident I've made the right choice. I notice, however, that the two routes seem to be going in almost opposite directions and wonder why that is. After walking for some time along the flat roadway, a car pulls up beside me with an older couple inside. The woman asks if I'm a peregrino, and when I say I am she tells me I'm going the wrong way and I need to turn around. I explain that I'm taking a different way, and everything is fine, but she insists I'm going the wrong way. The man even gets out of the car to show me the direction I need to be going in.

After much gesturing and (almost) yelling on their part, I agree to turn around even though I think they're wrong. I'm not following my gut and am angry that I'm following their advice when they obviously don't know about the alternate path I'm taking. Sure enough, the way they insisted I go is the rocky, hilly one I was trying to avoid. Now I'm even more angry. I know they meant well, but why were they so insistent? And why didn't I follow my feelings? As I search for the lesson in all of this, I start to notice how beautiful the views are, which I wouldn't have seen if I'd gone the other way. Maybe there's a reason why I'm taking this way after all.

As I leave a quaint little village, I notice a kitten on the trail up ahead following another pilgrim. The kitten has trouble keeping up and is crying its little heart out. Eventually it stops trying to follow the woman, and when I pass by it starts following me. I stop to give it some love and it can't get enough attention from me as it tries to climb up my leg. I tell it to go home as I turn to keep walking. It tries to keep up with me on the rocky trail, crying all the way. Eventually it stops and just sits down, wailing like a dying calf in a snowstorm! My heart breaks as I keep walking away, while my mind wonders if I should help it. I can't see any houses nearby, and I don't know if the kitten would allow me to carry it. Would anyone take it from me? As I've stated before, animals don't seem to be treated the same way here as we treat them in the U.S. The kitten's crying fades as I get farther and farther away, and now I'm crying. I hope I did the right thing.

It's another long day and I find myself walking alone for many miles. Perhaps to get my mind off the kitten, I start thinking of the craziest things. For instance, I start practicing (out loud no less), the "father of the bride" speech I'll give at my daughter's wedding. She isn't even engaged, and I have no idea if, or when, she'll get married, but I might as well start practicing what I'd like to say. This is what walking in the sun for hours at a time will do to your brain. It's a lovely speech, and of course I start to cry just thinking about it, and then something interesting happens. I realize that the perfect "father of the bride" speech will be to simply speak from my heart when the moment comes. No planning or rehearsing will be necessary. What is happening to the guy who always prepares and plans for everything?

The Camino is opening my heart. I didn't know my heart needed opening, but it feels wonderful. It's been such a strange day in this regard. I let go of my need to know where I was headed to today, but then I didn't follow my feelings when the locals insisted that I turn around. I felt cold-hearted when I left the crying kitten behind, and then my heart filled with joy thinking about my daughter's (potential) wedding day. *The Camino is a roller coaster in every way… and I'm grateful* for the experience.

My walking comes to an end at a welcoming hostel, and another wonderful communal dinner with pilgrims from Australia, Austria, Korea, Germany, and America. The woman from Australia has had a difficult year and she's walking the Camino to fix her life. Her fiancé called off their engagement and she was fired from her job. She's a bit jaded and doesn't believe that anyone walking the Camino is really a pilgrim; rather, we're all just tourists. The juxtaposition of her feelings reminds me of myself. On the one hand, she believes the reason many women are walking the Camino by themselves is because men have messed them up and they need to put their lives back together. On the other hand, she offers to work on my blistered feet, even though I'm the gender she doesn't like currently.

She also shares a funny story about when she climbed a church bell tower a few days ago, not realizing the bells would ring while she was up there. They startled her and she yelled out, "Holy F**king Jesus Christ!" Realizing what she'd done, she followed that with, "Oh, Shit!"

By the way, I realized after studying my guidebook this evening that I *was* going the wrong way when the locals turned me around. *I have no idea where I would have wound up if they hadn't saved me from my own confident ignorance.* I belong to Mensa (the high IQ Society), but I'm often not as smart as I think I am.

Today was the first day it felt like Fall. As the leaves begin to fall from the trees, little bits of me are falling away, revealing my authentic self, flawed and glorious.

"Let this promise in me start,
like an anthem in my heart."
— "From Now On" (from The Greatest Showman)

WE'RE ALL RELATED

Camino Day 19

Las Herrerias to A Balsa

19 miles

8.5 hours

7:30am–4:00pm

It wasn't the distance that was difficult today, it was the changes in elevation. Early in the day, it took me about two hours to climb one of the steepest and longest climbs on the Camino. Later in the day I had a long and steep descent, and my legs didn't know what was happening! I wouldn't recommend doing both the climb and the descent in the same day, but this is what must be done when you only have 26 days to walk to Santiago.

With the days getting shorter, it's now common to start my day in the dark. As I leave the hostel this morning, I see more cows and horses getting up for the day than I do people on the trail. I need to stay alert to see the trail markers and to avoid falling on the uneven ground.

Today I cross into the Galicia region of Spain, which I have been looking forward to the entire journey. It's supposed to be greener and wetter than what I've experienced thus far. The Camino is also getting more crowded the closer I get to Santiago.

The pilgrims who are just starting out are walking with fresh legs and a lot of enthusiasm; I remind myself not to judge them for not being "real" pilgrims because they're only walking a portion of the Camino. Non-judgment is something I aspire to, but I'm not there yet. I do find, however, that *when I release judgments of any kind, I feel more at peace with the way things are.*

I have some interesting experiences in some of the small villages I walk through today. As I enter one of them, I move out of the way to avoid the "running of the cows." I often see cows being let out into the pastures early in the day, with herding dogs barking enthusiastically to direct them.

Whenever I see a fountain in the towns I pass through, I try to fill up my two water bottles. These aren't fountains as we think of them in the U.S.; the water is untreated and isn't always safe to drink. Often there isn't a sign indicating if it's potable, and I won't drink it if I don't know it's safe. I come to one today and an old woman is washing some clothing in the pool of water below the fountain. I ask her if it's safe to drink and she assures me the water is excellent! I also come across another old woman this morning who's standing outside of her home with a plate of fresh pancakes. She offers one to me in exchange for a donation, and I happily give her one because they smell delicious!

As I cross into Galicia, I pass two men who are walking the Camino with two dogs, one of which is a German Shepherd puppy with big ears it still needs to grow into! One of the men is pulling a utility wagon on wheels that I assume holds their provisions. I wonder how far they walk each day and how the dogs' paws can handle the rough terrain.

Rather than end my day in a larger town with many hostels and restaurants to choose from, I push a little further to avoid starting tomorrow morning with a large crowd. The hostel I select is a renovated farmhouse that is environmentally friendly and prepares vegetarian meals. There are two showers, one with hot water and one with only cold water (not sure why some-one would take a cold shower on purpose), and the pilgrims are required to use biodegradable soap, which is provided for us. There's also a nice dog that barks a greeting when I arrive and likes attention from the pilgrims. The owner is Dutch, and his wife is Italian. Having been to Italy and enjoyed it myself, I asked her if she misses living there. She said she misses two things, the food, and being able to speak Italian on a regular basis. What she doesn't miss is the traffic!

As we all sit down to eat, the two men with dogs arrive. Apparently, they don't need to stay at the hostel, but they'd like to take a shower if possible. Staying in hostels with animals is difficult, and they're accustomed to sleeping outside in a tent. I learn that they started the Camino with only the adult dog, and they found the abandoned (or lost) puppy along the way and unofficially adopted it. They have booties to protect the dogs' paws, and when the puppy gets tired of walking, they carry it.

The dinner conversation is robust, and with people from Australia, Austria, Germany, France, and the U.S., it continues to be one of my favorite things about the Camino. *We may appear to be different from one another in many ways, but I believe we're more alike than we realize.*

The world is a book and those
who do not travel read only one page."
— Saint Augustine

SOMETIMES I'M A JERK

Camino Day 20

A Balsa to Castromaior

30 miles

12 hours

8:00am–8:00pm

Pilgrims who want to obtain a *Compostela*, or certificate of completion of their pilgrimage to Santiago, must obtain a Pilgrim Passport, or *credencial*. As you make your way along the Camino you get your pilgrim passport stamped as proof you were there. Stamps can be obtained from albergues, churches, cafes, and other sites of interest.

You can receive a Compostela by walking only the last 100 kilometers (62 miles) of the Camino, and this last section of the trail tends to be more crowded because many people just walk the minimum amount required to get their certificate. I bring this up because today I will pass through the town of Sarria, which is the closest city to being 100km from Santiago. And I need my patience pills today.

My morning gets off to a rough start. I'm one of the first ones up and go into one of the two bathrooms to get ready to leave. The albergues require that you leave your shoes/boots by the front door and not walk around in them, so I only have socks on my feet. I step in a puddle of water (at least I hope it is water) that had leaked out of the shower area, and now I'll have to start my day with wet feet. Then I sit down on the toilet and hear a loud cracking sound. What now?! The toilet seat is made of wood, in fact, if it wasn't sitting on top of a toilet bowl, you'd think it was a work of art. Apparently, I've cracked it. That's just great. This isn't how I imagined starting my day. My nerves are a bit frayed already.

I walk for over five hours before stopping to sit down. During that time, I do a lot of thinking about the logistics of walking the extra 50 miles past Santiago to the coast. At my current pace I'll arrive in Santiago on a Saturday, and I've heard it's one of the biggest holiday weekends of the year, which means finding a place to stay in Santiago will be difficult and expensive. I may as well keep walking all the way to the "end of the world," and then I can take a bus back to Santiago, arriving there on the Monday after the holiday when things will have settled down. If this plan works, I'll still get back to Santiago one day ahead of my original plan and will have added another 50 miles to my walk. Wow. That didn't seem possible until now. My tendency to plan everything has evolved. I still plan, but not too far ahead. *I'm waiting for circumstances to dictate my options instead of trying to anticipate everything that lies ahead.* Cool.

I see some chickens crossing the road ahead of me today but don't get there quickly enough to ask them why they were crossing. I hear that question has been pondered for centuries.

Ha! I also stop at a café and almost lose my cool because of how long it takes to be served. The accumulated fatigue is affecting me; I'm more annoyed with little things than I was earlier on the Camino. For instance, some of the pilgrims who are just starting their Camino talk on their cell phones a lot or play music while walking the trail. What other people do shouldn't bother me, but it does, at least sometimes.

After over eleven hours of walking I wind up in a village that has two hostels. I go to the one that looks better to me and am told it is full. I go to the other one and it is also full. I now must walk to the next town and I hope I can find a bed there. Fortunately, it isn't too far away, and the hostel has plenty of room. The group of pilgrims who arrived before me have already started connecting with each other and are talking in the dining area. I'm tired, my feet are killing me, and I'm not mentally sharp enough to carry on a conversation. I mumble a few "hellos'" and make my way to the shower.

When I checked in to the hostel, the proprietor gave me a token and said, "This is for the shower." Showers have been an interesting experience along the Camino, but this is the strangest one of all. On the wall *outside* of the bathroom is the box you put the shower token into. Once you insert the token, you have two minutes until the water will automatically start coming out of the shower. Once the water starts you have six minutes until it shuts off. I've heard the average American takes 10-15 minutes to shower, so once I insert the token, I have two minutes to take my clothes off and select what body parts I will wash first in case I run out of time!

I wash my high-priority areas and shampoo my hair and the water is still running. I hesitate to put soap on any parts I skipped in the event the water turns off and I can't rinse off. Such a stressful shower experience!

I made peace with my pain today. I'm tired of thinking about it. My family is probably tired of hearing about it. And you may be tired of reading about it. It's a part of my Camino experience, and I'm not going to mention It again.

It's getting close to 10pm when I text my family to let them know where I wound up today. Moments later Jacki texts back and asks if we can talk. I suggest we talk tomorrow and am clueless that she *really* needs to talk to me. A couple of texts later I learn that her dad is in the hospital on hospice and she is in the car driving her mom home. It's lights out now in the hostel and everyone's in bed... Jacki says it's fine that we talk tomorrow, and I'm too insensitive to know it's *not* fine.

I can't sleep. I'm thinking about my father-in-law. I'm thinking about my mother-in-law. I'm thinking about Jacki, who's having to work through this without me. And my whole body is radiating heat as if I have a fever.

I should have called Jacki. I want to tell her how much I love her. It's too late now.

"Be kind, for everyone you meet is fighting a harder battle." — Plato

THE HEAVENS CRIED TODAY

Camino Day 21

Castromaior to Mato

12 miles

5.5 hours

8:00am–1:30pm

Before I left home, Jacki and I had talked about what we'd do if something happened to one of her parents, especially her father, who is 91. He didn't have any serious health problems, but at his age anything can happen. I visited my in-laws before leaving for Spain, and while he didn't know it, I spoke to him as if it was the last time I'd see him. At that time, Jacki and I decided that I would finish my Camino if something were to happen. I have a feeling that my father-in-law has passed away, but I won't know what's happening until I talk to Jacki later. Right now, it's 1am at home.

It rained heavily during the night and it's still raining as I head out this morning. Other than the storm I chose to walk through in the mountains, I haven't had to deal with rain on the Camino. I have plastic bags over my socks and a rain poncho that fits over my backpack, and hopefully I'll stay relatively dry. The trail conditions deteriorate quickly when it gets wet.

I catch up to a couple I met at the hostel last night (they were the first ones up and out the door this morning). They're from England and I tell them about the news I got last night before bed. We walk together for a long time, and even with the rain and the somber news from last night, I appreciate our conversation.

My physical and emotional energy is low today. I stop walking early because I just don't have the motivation to keep going. My efforts to stay dry were partially successful, but my money, passport, and pilgrim credential got wet even though they were in the pocket of my rain jacket.

It's now early morning at home and I text Jacki to tell her I can talk anytime. She calls me almost immediately and tells me her father died during the night, around the time I woke up today. We talk and cry, and she asks me if I'm okay. Am I okay?! What about her? She is so strong. I don't feel badly about not saying goodbye to my father-in-law because of the last visit we had, but I'm upset I'm not there for Jacki. She had to make difficult end-of-life decisions on his behalf, and I wasn't there for her. We discuss again whether I should come home or finish my trip and decide I should continue. I'm supposed to give the eulogy at his memorial service, and that can be postponed until I return. I think about all the family members who came together a few weeks ago, having no idea it would be the last time they'd see my father-in-law.

He was the closest thing to a father I've ever had. Rest in Peace Dad.

"Do not pity the dead, Harry. Pity the living, and, above all those who live without love."
– Dumbledore, Harry Potter and the Deathly Hallows

I LOST IT

Camino Day 22

Mato to Pedrouzo

29 miles

11.5 hours

6:15am–5:45pm

There wasn't any rain in the forecast, and of course it rained all day! I guess predicting weather in Spain is as difficult as it is at home. Hurricane Leslie, which formed in the north Atlantic Ocean almost three weeks ago, made an unusual turn and is the strongest cyclone to strike the Iberian Peninsula since 1842. This is affecting the weather along the Camino and bringing several rounds of precipitation and wind. I think back on some of the difficult sections of trail I've walked and can't imagine how much harder it would have been in wet and windy conditions.

I walk for 2½ hours in the dark this morning without seeing a single person. At one point I come to a fork in the road with no indication of which way to go, which means I'm probably not on the Camino any longer. I backtrack for a while, and sure enough, I had missed a marker in the dark and should have turned instead of continuing straight. I'm wearing my rain poncho, but it's hard to stay dry because it's being blown about, even over my head at times. The dark cloud cover dampens my mood but walking through the beautiful eucalyptus forests helps.

Around midday I meet up with a Canadian couple that I met at the hostel from two nights ago. Canadians have a reputation of being exceptionally nice, and that has certainly been my experience along the Camino. I walk with them for a while and enjoy our conversation. We discuss the challenges of raising children (they are both retired teachers), what we've experienced and gained from our time on the Camino, and the concept of "good enough." For those of us who are perfectionists (that's me), *good enough can sound like we're settling for less than we're capable of.* It can also relieve some of the pressure of trying to control things we can't control. This reminds me of the serenity prayer I've been wearing around my neck.

My destination today is Pedrouzo, and my guidebook tells me the Camino passes through the *outskirts* of the town. The town center is where the hostels are, and I must be careful not to miss the turn into town. Even knowing this, I cross the road I should have turned at and keep walking until I realize I should have arrived there already. I'm feeling good and wonder if I should just keep going, but the next town is over two hours away and it only has one hostel that can accommodate 34 people. Given how crowded things are getting along the trail, I call the hostel in the next town and am told they are full.

I turn around and make my way back into town. I find an albergue that has some availability; unfortunately, the place is crowded, only upper bunks are left, and everyone's wet belongings are spread out everywhere. After starting to settle in, I'm told they've opened the "attic" and I can sleep there if I'd like. I'll have to climb more stairs, but the attic has regular beds, and as of now there's only one other person up there, so it's worth moving my things. It's hot in the attic and there aren't many electrical outlets to share, but hopefully I've made the right choice and will sleep well. I'll arrive in Santiago tomorrow and want to get an early start, hopefully ahead of the crowd.

I'm now three days ahead of my original schedule!

It's still raining as I venture out to find some dinner. I saw a pizza place on my way in that was filled with customers, and I've missed eating pizza. It's inexpensive and the pizza is just a step above frozen pizza.

When I return to the albergue, what was a quiet attic is now filled with a group of friends from Spain, and from what I can tell, they want to celebrate the holiday weekend in a big way. Most of them leave for dinner and don't return by lights out at 10pm. I have trouble sleeping because I'm hot, and all the lights are on. The group doesn't return until midnight, and to their credit, they try to be quiet. A few moments later I hear some rustling next to me and open my eyes to see someone moving my things off the empty bed beside me to make room for someone they brought back with them.

I had set out my wet things so they would dry, and I typically lay out what I'll need in the morning, which allows me to quietly get ready while other people are still sleeping. Having someone move my belongings sent me into a rage and I lost it! I've been on my best behavior on this pilgrimage, trying to be a patient and compassionate pilgrim, and now the night before I arrive in Santiago I explode!

I raise my voice and tell them they should have more respect for other people. I exclaim that I've walked almost twelve hours today and need to get some sleep. I have no idea if they understand a word I'm saying and most of them seem to be stunned and are standing motionless, except for one young woman who keeps repeating, "I'm sorry. I'm sorry. I'm sorry."

Now that I've delivered a theatrical performance and raised my blood pressure, I can't get to sleep. I'm upset with myself, and the person sleeping next to me is snoring like a freight train. After struggling for a couple of hours, the only thing I can think to do is to get up and start walking.

It's 3:00am.

"Before you speak, ask yourself: is it kind, is it necessary, is it true, does it improve on the silence?"
— Sai Baba

SANTIAGO IS NOT THE END

Camino Day 23

Pedrouzo to Negreira

26 miles

12 hours

3:30am–3:30pm

I'm out the door by 3:30am and will walk for over four hours in darkness, mostly in the woods. At first, I'm a bit startled by the sounds of animals and their eyes reflecting the light from my headlamp, but I've spent many years running in the early morning darkness in forest preserves at home. This is a familiar environment to me.

In one of the villages I pass through, a cat comes out of nowhere and walks in front of me, as if it's leading the way out of town. It keeps up a quick pace until something else gets its attention, or maybe it thought its job was done and I had successfully found my way. I don't know why, but I'm feeling my father-in-law's presence this morning. Since his passing there have been several times that I felt him nearby, as if he's checking on me, and letting me know he's okay.

At 8:30am I arrive in Santiago. I want to see the famous cathedral which houses the remains of the Apostle Saint James and is the end point of The Way, but I won't go inside or attend the pilgrim's Mass today, because my pilgrimage is not over.

It's Saturday morning and the only people I see appear to be tour groups. I hear someone say something about a peregrino as I walk by. Yes, that would be me!

The cathedral's bells ring out at 9am but I have the hardest time finding it! You'd think a cathedral would be hard to miss, but you can't see anything other than the maze of buildings that surround it. When I arrive at the front of the cathedral I'm overcome with emotion. It's a lot to take in. *This has been extraordinarily hard, and I'm not done yet.*

After soaking in the magnitude of arriving in Santiago three days early, I'm off to get my Compostela at the *Oficina del Peregrino* (Pilgrim Office). There's a long line of people already waiting, but it only takes about thirty minutes to get through the queue.

I'd like to stay in Santiago, but I need to keep moving, and I'll be back in a couple of days. Finding the Camino Finisterre (the trail to Fisterra) is a little tricky, but a local woman gets me started in the right direction. There will be fewer pilgrims going on to Fisterra and I may have even more time alone on the trail. The next town is about six hours away. My guidebook only goes to Santiago, so I have very little information and no maps from this point forward.

As I leave Santiago, it feels like I've entered another region of Spain. It's much greener and there's even humidity in the air.

The ground is less rocky and it's sandier. The biggest change I notice is with the pilgrims themselves. Those who have made the commitment to go to the sea appear more determined and serious. They walk at a fast pace and look like seasoned hikers. *Am I one of them now?* Sometimes I see people coming the other way, those who have walked to Fisterra and are now coming back to Santiago. They have a peace and serenity about them that makes me want some of that!

After last night's fiasco at the hostel, I'm not sure I can stay at another one. I wasn't planning on staying in a hotel until I return to Santiago, and I think about what I'm willing to pay for the comforts of a hotel. The number 35 Euros comes to mind. As I get to the outskirts of Negreira, I start seeing advertisements along the trail for various hotels. One called Hotel Millan looks reasonable, and I stop there. I ask the woman at the front desk how much it costs for a room and she replies, "40 Euros, and that doesn't include dinner or breakfast." I say it's more than I want to pay and ask if there's a special rate for pilgrims. She looks me over and offers, "35 Euros including breakfast, but no dinner!" I hand over my credit card.

Later, I walk across the street to a gas station/convenience store to get some food for dinner. It's not fancy, but lunch meat, Doritos, Coke, and some chocolate do the trick. I'll need to walk another long day tomorrow, which will be three days in a row of ten hours or more. This will put me in position to finish early enough on my final day that I'll be able to catch the bus back to Santiago. Then I'll be able to spend two nights in a row at a hotel before leaving Spain. That sounds wonderful, but I still have work to do and can't get caught up in thinking too far ahead. I'm getting better at *spontaneous planning.*

"It is good to have an end to journey towards;
but it is the journey that matters, in the end."
— Ursula K. Le Guin

I CAN SEE THE BARN

Camino Day 24

Negreira to Cee

32 miles

13 hours

7:30am–8:30pm

Today is my longest day in distance and time, and oddly enough, my most enjoyable day of walking. When I was young and lived on a farm, I often rode a pony named Lady. I usually rode bareback, and Lady had a habit of finding ways of getting me off her back, usually by coming to an abrupt stop while galloping, then watching as I flew over her head and landed on the ground. Hopefully my abrupt stop in Fisterra tomorrow won't be a rough landing!

When I'd take Lady for long rides, as soon as she could see the farm on the way back, she'd suddenly want to gallop like the wind (which could also make me fall off!). I'm kind of feeling like Lady today. I can almost see the "barn" and I'm antsy to get to the finish.

Since the terrain is softer now, I go back to my original shoes, and I've already torn a hole in the top of the new shoes I bought in Leon. It rains all morning, but I've started accepting the weather conditions, no matter what they are. At home I often obsess over the weather forecasts.

I take an alternate route that didn't look like it would be as difficult as the official trail, but it's poorly marked, and I don't know if I'm on the right path for a lot of it. At one point I see a dog running around and wonder if it's with someone, then I see two men with big rifles who are hunting. The dog is supposed to retrieve whatever they shoot.

I spend A LOT of time by myself today. While I reflect on my journey along the Camino, I realize I've experienced and learned things that could be helpful to others. As a speaker/trainer by profession, it's not unusual for me to think about how I can share my knowledge with others. Some ideas for keynote speeches come together in my mind. I am even able to talk them through since no one is around to hear me.

Late in the day I start a four-hour stretch in nothing but wilderness. It is a beautiful area, which I don't fully appreciate because of the sound of gunshots around me. It is the most con-cerned I've been for my safety on the entire Camino. I'm not a hunter, and it's hard for me to tell how close they are to me. At one point I come across a hunter with his dog and he says some-thing about my being on the Camino so late in the day. Perhaps it is unusual for pilgrims to be on the trail this late?

It's dark when I get to the town of Cee… a great name for a town that gives me my first glance at the Atlantic Ocean! I'd pre-fer to stay at a hotel, but I can't find one along the main road I'm walking on, and it's difficult to find my way in the dark. I find a hostel that seems nice enough and hope for the best. It's the most uncomfortable bed I've slept on yet, but it doesn't matter. Tomorrow I reach the ocean and my long walk is over.

As I near the finish line, I contemplate on how this experience has affected me. I'd like to think that I've changed in beneficial ways, and that my behaviors will reflect these changes. At the same time, old habits are hard to break. Hopefully "the Camino will interfere" and will give me what I *need*, which may not necessarily be what I'm looking for.

"Change in your behavior may allow others to like you better, but in and of themselves, behaviors do not make you a better person." – John G. Blumberg

FINISH WHAT YOU START

Camino Day 25

Cee to Fisterra

10 miles

3.5 hours

7:00am–10:30am

One of the random, but interesting memories I have of my father-in-law is the time we were under the house in the crawl space, and we saw a salamander. Salamanders are not common in our area, and my father-in-law's reaction was that it was something you don't want under your house and it should be killed. I suggested we try to catch it in a bucket in order to set it free in the woods behind the house. He probably questioned my desire to keep it alive, but he respected it and we did just that. My father-in-law has been on my mind a lot as I've gotten close to the end of my Camino. He would have questioned my desire to do the Camino, but he would have respected it, and deep down I believe he would be cheering me on to finish what I started, and he'd be proud of the accomplishment.

Yesterday was my longest day. Today is my shortest day. It's only a few hours to the trail marker that reads Km 0,000 (the markers have been counting down along the way). The weather, however, is the worst I've experienced on the trip. It's raining heavily and the wind is picking up… my rain poncho won't do much to keep me, or my possessions, dry. Who cares? It's the last day, and I'd crawl to the end on my hands and knees if I had to.

Easier said than done. Walking in the pouring rain in the dark isn't much fun, and it's hard to see the trail markings. Much of the trail is on roadways today and I want to make sure the traffic sees me along the shoulder. While climbing a particularly steep hill, I'm frustrated and discouraged by the conditions (just yesterday I had accepted the weather… the roller coaster continues). For some reason, I happen to look down directly in front of me and I come to a halt. My headlamp is shining light on something I haven't seen since many years ago in the crawl space under the house… a salamander. It stays put for a moment, giving me time to realize what's happening, and then it moves off the trail.

That was my father-in-law, encouraging me and reminding me to stop complaining about my circumstances. Finish, and get back home to your family, he would have said. I'm too wet to notice the tears running down my cheeks.

Eventually, the trail is under water, and there's no way I can keep my feet dry. I have no concern for myself or my belongings at this point, just a singular goal… get to the lighthouse at the end of the world. And if I take too long to get there, I'll miss the bus back to Santiago and will have to spend the night in Fisterra, which I'd prefer not to do.

Fisterra is also known as Finisterre. I've chosen to refer to it as Fisterra because that's the Galician spelling. It's a seaside town that's all abuzz this Monday morning, and I need to get though the town to take the only road out to the lighthouse, which is a couple of miles outside of town. Along the way I see a statue honoring the pilgrims who make this journey. I haven't seen anyone else on the trail today, but I know millions of people have walked to Santiago, and many of them have continued to the sea.

I'm exhausted, I'm soaking wet, and the clouds and fog are so thick I can't see more than a hundred feet in front of me. I can hear the ocean, but I can't see it... and then I see the lighthouse. I've done it. I've walked 550 miles in 25 days, averaging 22 miles and 9 hours of walking every day. I'm blessed. I'm thankful. I miss and appreciate Jacki and my family more than I can put into words. Many people were supporting me with their thoughts and prayers, and in this moment, it's overwhelming.

I stand in the rain taking it all in and record a selfie video to capture exactly what I'm feeling. It's a short recording, because I can't linger too long... I have a bus to catch, and it's a two mile walk back into town.

The bus "station" is a large crowd of people on the sidewalk, waiting for the bus to arrive. I don't see any way to buy a ticket. I guess you do that on the bus? The crowd is getting larger by the minute; I hope it's a big bus!

It is. We're not allowed to take our backpacks on the bus, they're supposed to be put in storage areas that you access from the outside. With so many pilgrims returning to Santiago, the pile of backpacks is substantial and they're all just tossed into the storage compartment. It isn't until I board the bus that I realize that everything I brought to Spain, except my phone and the clothes I'm wearing, I had put into my backpack to stay dry. That means my passport, credit cards, and all my money (except the small amount I used to pay for my ticket) are in there as well. The bus will make several stops before reaching Santiago and I won't be able to see if my belongings remain safely stored.

The only thing I've had to eat all day is one soda and two energy bars, and now I must endure a three-hour bus ride. It's the first time I've been on anything that moves since I started walking the Camino over three weeks ago, and I'm not enjoying it. I'm hungry, tired, sad, wet and worried about my belongings. This isn't how I imagined things would go on my last day of walking. I almost want to ask the driver to pull over so I can walk back to Santiago, but I'd miss my flight home, and *I'm ready to go home.*

After arriving in Santiago and retrieving my backpack, I walk to my hotel, which occupies a building that was once the Oblatas Convent. They even upgraded me to a suite that has a view of the cathedral. I get out of my wet clothes, take a shower, and shave off my Camino beard. I've never let my beard grow this long and I had no idea how hard it would be to shave it off with just a regular razor. The hairs are long, and it takes a long time, but when I'm done I feel like I'm starting the transformation back to my "normal" self. I look younger without the facial hair, but I looked more at peace with it.

I spend some time walking around Santiago. There's a steady stream of pilgrims who are just arriving, and probably going no further. Some are reuniting with friends and people they met along the way, and there's lots of hugs, tears, and smiles. In my wanderings I come across the Canadian couple I'd walked with several days ago; they've just arrived and are enjoying some dinner. We chat a few minutes and they invite me to join them, but I'm not in the mood and graciously decline.

I don't know how to feel right now. I should be ecstatic and relieved, but I feel sad and out of place. The mix of emotions is all over the place. All I know to do is to keep walking. I circle the outside of the cathedral several times, each time seeing new people arriving. The two men with the dogs arrive and the crowd in the square goes wild! They touched many people as they traveled the Camino, and everyone is happy to see that they've arrived safely. The older dog looks exhausted and lies down amidst all the commotion. The puppy is alert and curious but takes his place on the ground next to his "big brother."

I explore the inside of the cathedral a bit, knowing I'll spend a lot more time there tomorrow. Eventually I get some dinner and go back to the hotel. It has been an emotionally exhausting day.

Oh, and that video I took at the lighthouse? It's gone. I assume the screen wasn't responding to my fingers because everything was wet. Or maybe there's more woo-woo going on.

"The secret is not following the right path;
it's following that right path to the end.
Don't quit, my friend, until you've arrived."
— Toni Sorenson

HAPPY BIRTHDAY

Today is my 54th birthday! My body feels the accumulated fatigue of over 500 miles of walking, and I move around my hotel room like someone who's much older than 54. Today is also the first day in the last twenty-five days that I don't have to get up and get walking. What will I do instead?

The pilgrim's Mass is at noon and I'd like to see the cathedral beforehand, so I get there around 9:30am. It's enormous, as many cathedrals in Europe are, and there are many areas to explore inside. There are also a lot of tourists there, doing what tourists do, like taking pictures where cameras aren't allowed, touching what shouldn't be touched, and making a lot of noise while posing in front of everything. God, I miss the trail!

I pay my respects to the remains of Saint James and say a prayer of thanks for my safe journey along the Camino. I felt protected out there, even when I was alone for hours in remote areas. I trusted that no harm would come to me if I stayed focused on my intentions and respected the people, the animals, and the land I walked upon.

By 10:30am the cathedral is crowded, and people start to sit in the pews waiting for the Mass at noon. I find a place to sit with a good view and I just relax, something I haven't done much of for a while. I recognize some of the people coming in from my earlier days on the trail, wondering how they fared and glad to see they made it to Santiago. The atmosphere is like a reunion and the gathering crowd is often reprimanded by the cathedral staff to lower our voices. We are in a church after all.

The Mass is moving even though I don't understand a word of it. One of the highlights that people come to see is near the end, the swinging of the giant incense burner. The ritual requires at least a half dozen attendants to perform it. It's quite a sight to see, and even though you're not supposed to take pictures or record it, many people do, and you can find them online. Here's a good one: https://youtu.be/7yIRVzR-3K0 . I sit to the side of the altar in the second row, and the burner went right over my head every time it passes by. Amazing.

After Mass I purchase some gifts to take home, do my laundry, and spend the rest of the day relaxing… off my feet. I feel like I'm re-entering the world again. The best part of my birthday was talking to Jacki, even though we spent a lot of time working out the details for her dad's memorial service.

My regular life is coming back into focus, and that's okay.

"The meaning of life is to find your gift.
The purpose of life is to give it away."
— Pablo Picasso

SUCCESS
INCLUDES SUBTRACTION

I start my trip home today, but not until this afternoon. I reflected a lot on my experiences of the last few weeks before going to bed last night and ended up having a lot of "Camino dreams" during the night.

I'm walking more normally today, which is a good sign. I don't expect my feet to fully heal for several weeks, maybe longer. The hotel has a great breakfast, and being a Marriott property, there are several Americans staying here. When you travel abroad, you can pick out the Americans easily because many of them fit the stereotype of being loud, demanding, and uninterested in blending in and learning the local customs. Even something as simple as learning a few basic phrases in the local language goes a long way in building rapport with people. I notice several Americans at breakfast complaining about how things are different here, while making no attempts to use Spanish words when ordering their food. Am I being judgmental? Perhaps a little.

How is it that I was able to do in 25 days what most people take much longer to do? Was it my resolve? I'm sure that played a part. The best definition of resolve I've ever heard is to *promise yourself to never give up*. That sounds like willpower, but willpower is limited and temporary; it only lasts so long. That said, what was my formula for success?

Subtraction. For most of my life I thought the formula for success involved addition. And when you're young, perhaps you can keep adding things to your plate, but I think we reach a point when our plates are full, and we can't add anything more without stuff falling off. I can remember as a child being at the grocery store with my mom and not having enough money to pay for all the items in the shopping cart. What do you take out? The milk? The bread? The meat? It all feels necessary. I think life is like that. Everything feels necessary, so we keep adding and accumulating things, but we still don't feel like we're able to manage it all.

The only way I was able to accomplish what I did was to take almost everything else out of my shopping cart. I only had to focus on, and take care of, myself. I woke up every day and I walked. Rinse and repeat. No distractions. Almost no technology. Everything you need is on your back. *You can do a lot when you clear the clutter from your life.*

I was also reminded of how much we need each other, even to accomplish personal goals. A simple "Buen Camino" was enough for me to pick up the pace and forget about the pain. *I don't believe anything worthwhile is accomplished alone.* There was an energy, even a love, on the Camino that all the pilgrims gave to, and received from, each other. The difference between the words "alone" and "all one" is adding another "L." And I believe the additional "L" is love. And I don't believe the opposite of love is hate, I believe it's fear. *Fear makes us feel that we are alone. Love makes us feel we are all one. We don't need higher walls that divide us, we need longer tables that join us.*

I'll get off my soapbox now.

The travel logistics today won't be pleasant. Hotel checkout time is 2pm, but my flight to Paris isn't until 7pm, so I'll have several hours of waiting at the airport. I'll arrive in Paris at 9pm and will take a shuttle to my hotel. Tomorrow morning it's back to the airport for my flight to Chicago. This all seems complicated compared to my pilgrimage.

That's the funny thing about transformative experiences. It isn't hard to feel changed and renewed when you take some time to unplug and get away from your normal routines. *The challenge is staying transformed when you come down from the mountaintop and return to your normal life.*

"When you say no to something, you're saying yes to what matters most." – Neen James

HOMECOMING

Nothing like jumping right into the craziness of life!

The Charles de Gaulle airport is in a state of chaos this morning because one of the terminals is on lockdown due to a security issue. It's the terminal I need to get to. Adding to the confusion are the airport security guards shouting at people in French when thousands of international travelers don't understand what's being said. Eventually the chaos subsides, and my flight isn't even delayed.

It's a long flight home and I think about the intentions I set at the beginning of this journey:

Surrender

I was able to let go of my need to control and plan for every contingency. I've learned how to successfully make plans with information as it comes instead of trying to think too far ahead (*spontaneous planning*). It's not like I'm a completely different person, but I've made progress with this intention and feel a bit lighter (metaphorically and physically) after leaving my stone at Cruz de Ferro and releasing my need to understand everything. I'm learning to tap into my feelings, to listen more to my heart and less to my head.

Sacrifice

No revelations surfaced as to how I can be of greater service and give more of myself for the benefit of others. I feel more drawn to issues of social justice, but don't yet know how that will manifest into action. I do feel more at peace with my ability to make a positive impact in others' lives through my speaking and training. As Albert Schweitzer said, "The only one among you who will be truly happy are those who have found how to serve."

Storyline

Especially on the days I walked the Meseta, I spent a lot of time thinking about my life experiences, looking for patterns and lessons. While there are many phases in a given lifetime, it seems like I'm entering a *major* phase of change and transformation. I can't see ahead to know what this means, but it's exciting to think about what that might bring, like a chrysalis becoming a butterfly!

Suffering

I asked for it, and I got it! I've said enough about this already, but one realization is that this experience reaffirmed, at least for me, that transformation requires discomfort. The times I gained the most insight were often the times I pushed myself beyond reasonable limits, whether it was walking into stormy weather or getting up at 3am to start walking. I could have waited for the weather to pass, or slept in, but it wouldn't have been the same experience.

Spiritual

Perhaps the greatest thing about the entire pilgrimage was feeling my heart open. I experienced feelings, emotions, and even thoughts at a deeper level than I have before. I don't know if my heart will stay open when I return to my normal life, but I'm hoping it does at least a little bit. If nothing else, I'll remember what it felt like and it should be easier to open in the future. Getting lids off jars is always easier once the seal has been broken.

I realize at a deep level that *many of the concerns of life don't matter nearly as much as we think they do.* My family survived in my absence. The company I work for is doing just fine without me. Even the NFL was able to start the football season without my being able to watch a single game.

You don't have to walk 500 miles across Spain to get some of these insights, but it's the path I chose.

I had told Jacki not to come meet me at the airport. I'd take a taxi home. I knew I'd be emotional when I saw her and wanted our reunion to be at home and not at the airport. I missed her immensely and am extremely appreciative of the sacrifices she made for me to do this. Hopefully I'm a better husband and father as a result.

Walking in the front door, I give her a huge hug, and it doesn't take long for us to pick up where we left off. There's a lot going on at home right now and it's time for me to be involved. All the work that's been done on our home while I was away looks great, and she's done such an amazing job managing things on her own.

I didn't sleep on the flight home, and once again I've been up for over 24 hours before I finally go to sleep.

Showering in my own shower and sleeping in my own bed never felt so good.

"A man travels the world over in search of what he needs and returns home to find it." – George A. Moore

BUEN CAMINO

Home. It's good to be home. And a part of me misses the way of the Camino. The overall feeling that remains is gratitude. There are many things I've expressed my thankfulness for while on the Camino, and there are countless more, including:

- My knees didn't complain once. I've had knee problems in the past, and many pilgrims were dealing with knee issues.

- I didn't suffer any illness. Many pilgrims became ill from food, water, or the harsh conditions, but I was spared.

- No bed bugs. Bed bugs can be a problem along the Camino, but I had no issues.

There are things I'm proud of:

- I didn't fall, not once. My walking poles saved me many times (and I had to be persuaded by my family to even bring them).

- I didn't get hopelessly lost. The few times I got off course, I recovered quickly.

- I crushed my original goal! I didn't let pain or fatigue slow me down.

For future pilgrims, my quick advice and suggestions:

- Take more time than I did. I wouldn't recommend my pace to anyone.

- Learn some Spanish. Locals can enrich the experience, if you're able to talk to them!

- Don't plan too much. Be open to taking each day as it comes.

I know I will never forget my Camino experience and I see my life now as AC/BC. I'm committed to keeping the AC (After Camino) Blaine alive, trying to resist the old habits and routines that will take me back to who I was BC (Before Camino).

Re-entering "normal" life is now upon me. It's a day of "firsts" for me today:

- First day back to work (my email inbox is overflowing!).

- First day running in over a month (it went better than I thought it would).

- First day driving a car in over a month (kind of like riding a bike, you don't forget how to do it).

As I take each day, one day at a time, as I did in Spain, it is my vow to keep alive the attitude and essence of the Camino.

In my Pilgrim Passport, the following were listed as the Spirit of the Camino:

- Live in the Moment

- Welcome Each Day – Its Pleasures and Its Challenges

- Make Others Feel Welcome

- Share

- Feel the Spirit of Those Who Have Come Before You

- Imagine Those Who Will Follow You

- Appreciate Those Who Walk with You Today

These ideas are simple, but not easy. I plan to work on them one at a time, perhaps taking a different one each day of the week, then repeating them the next week until the new habits start to stick.

As I mentioned earlier, I carried my father's one-year AA medallion around my neck for the entire Camino. My parents got divorced when I was one year old, and I didn't get reacquainted with my father until I was a teenager. I didn't develop a friendship with him until I was an adult and had started my own family. Fortunately, I got the best years of his life, when he was sober.

Every year on his birthday, I listen to a recording he made at an AA meeting when he talked about his journey to sobriety. He says something at the end of his talk that I find profound:

"I'm not the person I used to be.

I'm not the person I want to be.

But I'm happy with who I am today."

In thinking about my journey along the *Camino de Santiago*:

I'm not the person I used to be.

I'm not the person I want to be.

But I'm happy with who I am today.

Do *you* like going for long walks?

Buen Camino.

"As you travel through life, offer good wishes to each being you meet." – Buddha

Thank you for reading my book, *From Sore Soles to a Soaring Soul.*

Like the Camino, writing the book was quite a journey and a labor of love.

I hope you enjoyed reading it.

I would deeply appreciate if you would leave a review on Amazon with your honest opinion and the appropriate number of stars.

Thank you, and Buen Camino!

Blaine A. Rada

blaine@blainerada.com

ABOUT THE AUTHOR

Blaine Rada's travels and adventures started early. Between kindergarten and high school, he lived in eight places, attended eight different schools, and spent three years at a "free school," which encouraged independent learning, where Blaine focused on art, math, and playing in the mud.

Smart enough to be a member of Mensa, Blaine still will do things that don't make any sense, like the time he chained his bike to a concrete post, not realizing it could simply be lifted off because the post was only four feet tall.

Blaine was named "America's Greatest Thinker" in 2005 by winning The Great American Think-Off, a national philosophy competition. He won the event arguing that cooperation benefits society more than competition. Kind of ironic. (More information on this event can be found at www.thinkoff.org.)

As a teenager, Blaine discovered his life mission was to have a positive impact on as many people as possible. Even then, he knew it would involve professional speaking. As a member of the National Speakers Association, Blaine has achieved the highest earned designation, the CSP, or Certified Speaking Professional.

Blaine has spent over 30 years in the financial services industry and travels the country helping companies grow their business and stand out from the competition.

Blaine would love to hear from you! If you have comments about this book, questions about the Camino de Santiago, or just want to say "Buen Camino!," write to blaine@blainerada.com.